GW00676458

# THE ELIZABETHAN TOWER OF LONDON

## The Haiward and Gascoyne plan of 1597

# THE ELIZABETHAN TOWER OF LONDON

## The Haiward and Gascoyne plan of 1597

*By*

ANNA KEAY

*London Topographical Society*
*Publication No. 158*
*with*
*Historic Royal Palaces*
*and*
*The Society of Antiquaries of London*
2001

London Topographical Society
Hon. Editor: Ann Loreille Saunders, PhD, FSA



Publication No. 158 of the
London Topographical Society
3 Meadway Gate, London NW11

ISBN 0 902087 44 4

PRODUCED IN GREAT BRITAIN BY
OUTSET SERVICES LTD, BOSTON SPA, WEST YORKSHIRE

# CONTENTS

# LIST OF ILLUSTRATIONS

# INTRODUCTION

No work on the Tower of London is complete without a plate of the Haiward and Gascoyne survey of 1597. Preceding by eighty-five years the next plan to show anything like the same level of detail, Haiward and Gascoyne's work constitutes the only survey of the Tower of London before it underwent substantial renovation in the course of the seventeenth century. In particular, it is the only measured visual source for the complex of buildings in the Inmost Ward which formed the royal residential area of the palace; indeed, with the exception of one fifteenth-century illuminated manuscript, it is the only visual source of any description dedicated to depicting the Tower of London in detail before the Civil War.[i]

Although the principal seventeenth-century plans of the Tower of London have received valuable attention, no critical study has yet been made of this extraordinarily important sixteenth-century survey.[ii] This is no doubt partly because the original version of Haiward and Gascoyne's plan has not been seen by any scholar for over 250 years and the survey is known only from copies made in the eighteenth century. Therefore, all our faith in this extremely important survey rests, not on the original document, or any contemporary preparatory drawings, but on eighteenth-century copies about the status of which precious little has been established.[iii]

This study investigates the reasons for which the plan was made, the fate of the original, the origins of the existing versions, the accuracy of the survey and its importance as a source for the history of the Tower.

## NOTES

[i] See, for example, the extent to which the Haiward and Gascoyne plan has informed H. Colvin (ed.), *The History of the King's Works*, 6 vols. (London, 1962–82), II, pp. 262–77; R. Allen Brown and P. Curnow, *Tower of London* (London, 1984); G. Parnell, *The Tower of London* (London, 1993); S. Thurley, 'Royal lodgings at The Tower of London 1216–1327', *Architectural History* 38 (1995), pp. 36–57; and the section on the royal lodgings at the Tower in S. Thurley, *The Royal Palaces of Tudor England* (New Haven and London, 1993), pp. 32–4.

[ii] G. Parnell, 'Five seventeenth-century plans of the Tower of London', *London Topographical Record* XXV (1985), pp. 63–82.

[iii] The complexities of the story of the survey have often been obscured by misleading labels: for example, a coloured version of the eighteenth-century engraving is called simply 'Plate of the Tower in 1597 (Hayward and Gascoigne)', in J. Charlton (ed.), *The Tower of London: its Buildings and Institutions* (London, 1978), plate 8, disguising the fact that it is actually at several removes from the work of Haiward and Gascoyne. Until recently almost the only properly labelled reproduction of the survey was in Colvin (ed.), *The History of the King's Works*, II, plate 45; though in the text Colvin and Summerson say of the royal palace as shown on the plan, 'the only buildings which are identified by name are the hall, the queen's (i.e. the king's) lodgings, the queen's (i.e. the king's) gallery and the Wardrobe'; while, in fact, the wardrobe is not identified, and the jewel house is: ibid., III, p. 266.

# ACKNOWLEDGEMENTS

Many people have contributed in a wide range of ways to the publication of this slim volume, and I am extremely grateful to them for their assistance. Among those who have been kind enough to discuss and correspond with me on various aspects of the Haiward and Gascoyne plan are: Peter Barber of the British Library Maps Department; Sarah Bendall of Merton College, Oxford; Mrs Edward Brudenell; His Grace the Duke of Buccleuch; A. Fisher, archivist at Drumlanrig Castle; Christine Hiskey, archivist at Holkham Hall; Rose Mitchell of the PRO; Stephen Priestley; Derek Renn; Heidi Taylor; Susan Tomkins, archivist at Beaulieu; Rachel Watson of the Northampton Record Office, and the staff of the National Register of Archives. Clare Murphy and Ann Saunders marshalled the illustrations and edited the text. Geoffrey Parnell, Keeper of Tower History, discussed the plan with me at length, shared a wealth of useful references and has read the text in draft. The eleventh-hour hunt for the Whitehand copy would not have been successful without the help of Simon Thurley. Jeremy Ashbee read the text in several drafts, discussed endless details with great patience and shared with me his own work on the Tower with characteristic generosity. Edward Impey first pointed out the need for a thorough examination of the 1597 survey, drew up the plan of the fortress opposite page 4, has commented painstakingly on the text and is in no small part responsible for it reaching publication. The Society of Antiquaries generously allowed me access to their library, waived their reproduction fees and gave financial support to the publication.

ANNA KEAY

# EDITOR'S NOTE

The London Topographical Society is delighted to co-operate with Historic Royal Palaces in the publication of this thorough and scholarly examination of the 1597 plan of the Tower of London. The Society is grateful to the Society of Antiquaries of London for permission to reproduce their copy of the plan, and for a generous grant towards the cost of production.

Especial thanks are due to Clare Murphy, Historic Royal Palaces; this volume owes much to her editorial expertise, her steady patience and her ability to procure photographs and permissions for reproduction with uncommon speed.

ANN SAUNDERS

# I. THE EXTANT COPIES

THE survey of 1597 exists today in four main copies made in the space of forty years; two of these are connected with the Society of Antiquaries and are relatively well known, while the other two, which are in the Public Record Office (PRO), have been almost completely ignored. The most frequently reproduced copy of the plan is an engraving published by the Society of Antiquaries which bears the date 1742 (Fig. 1) and the title: 'A True and Exact Draught of the TOWER LIBERTIES, survey'd in the Year 1597 by GULIELMUS HAIWARD and J. GASCOYNE'.[1] Less frequently cited is a pen and ink drawing on paper with colour washes in the collection of the Society of Antiquaries (Col. Pl. 1) which describes itself as a 'copy' of the 'draught of the TOWER LIBERTIES' of 1597, but which is, itself, undated.[2]

Of the two copies in the PRO, one is a pen and ink drawing with vivid colour washes (Col. Pl. 3); the information on this reveals that it was not made directly from the original, but that it was the work of one J. Heath in 1752, who was himself working from a copy of the sixteenth-century original taken by C. Lemprière in 1741.[3] The second PRO copy is also pen and ink with washes, though now faded (Col. Pl. 2); it is entitled: '... Coppy of the draught of the TOWER LIBERTIES Survey'd in the year 1597 by GULIELMUS HAIWARD and I. GASCOYNE Coppied Ianuary 1712 by Robert Whitehand'.[4] The relationship between the known Society of Antiquaries' copies has always been somewhat unclear, while the importance — indeed the existence — of the other two versions has gone unappreciated.[5]

## Origins: The Society of Antiquaries' copies

The minutes of the Society of Antiquaries shed considerable light on the history of the two copies associated with that institution (Fig. 2). On Thursday 21 May 1741 the Society's engraver, George Vertue, showed the Society 'a Curious illuminated Drawing on a Large Imperial Sheet of paper of the Tower libertys, containing the Tower & all the fortifications & Works Survey'd in the Year 1597 by William Hayward & John Gascoyne with Alphabetical references to the several Towers & gates'. This drawing, which had been 'brought from' the Duke of Montagu, excited considerable attention among the Antiquaries, who immediately 'Agreed That with his Grace's permission a drawing be taken thereof for this Society's use'.[6] By the next meeting, a week later, the Duke had given his consent. The copy (Col. Pl. 1), which measures 72.5 cm by 52 cm, was made over the summer of 1741 and at the meeting on 3 September 1741 'Mr Vertue according to an order of the Society brought an illuminated drawing or Plan of the Tower of London'; by this time the original had apparently already been returned. So impressed were the Antiquaries that at that very meeting 'it was moved & seconded that wheras the Plan is very Curious & Singular wether [*sic*] it might be engraved'.[7] Accordingly, just over a year later, in September 1742, George Vertue presented the engraving (Fig. 1) for the Society's approval and on 30 September it was 'order'd that M$^{r}$ Vertue deliver three copies to each member as usual'.[8]

Therefore, it seems that the drawing was made before the engraving, taken directly from the original and intended 'for this Society's use'. The engraving was made afterwards, once the original had been returned, and was commissioned for distribution to the members of the Society because of the 'curious and singular nature' of the survey. This is borne out by the appearance of the two: the drawing is more detailed in the areas where the two disagree;[9] and while the drawing is quite simple in presentation, the engraving features elaborate, characteristically mid-eighteenth-century cartouches and scrolls, which were presumably added to make the survey more attractive to the Antiquaries for whom it was intended.[10] Having said that, there are some embellishments on the drawing, but these are restricted to the body of the plan, while the appended information is simply presented in boxes. Similarly, the fact that 'the Remains of ye Royal Palace' is included in the subtitle of the engraving, but is not mentioned in the subtitle to the drawing, would suggest that the presentation of the plan in the engraving had been slightly tuned to excite the interest of its prospective audience.

Both the drawing and the engraving are unsigned. The obvious assumption is that they were the work of Vertue himself, who was the Society's engraver and who clearly co-ordinated the whole operation of borrowing and copying the plan in Montagu's possession. However, Vertue usually signed the work he undertook for the Society and

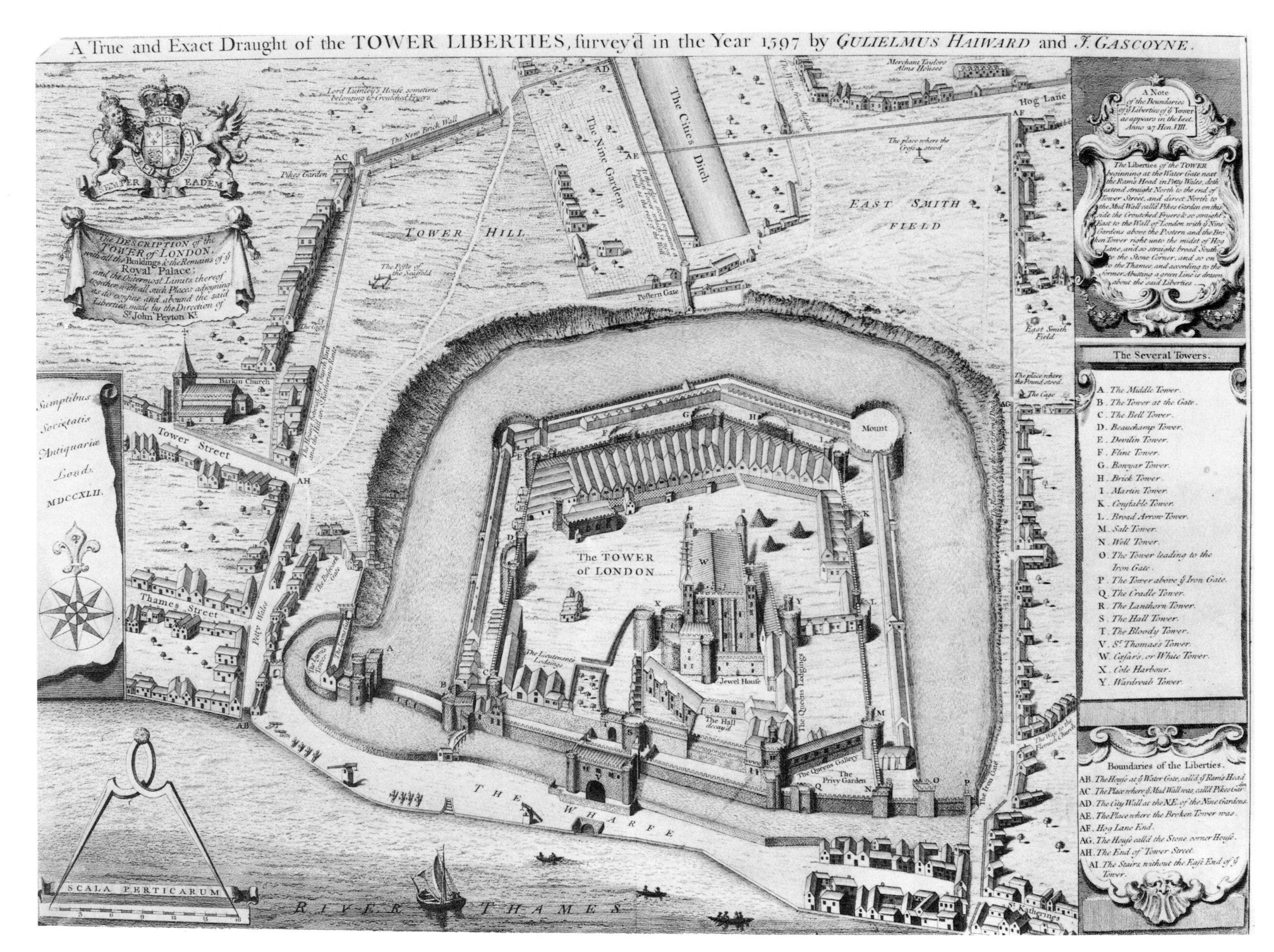


Fig. 1. Engraving of colour plate 1 made for the Society of Antiquaries in 1742. (© Historic Royal Palaces)

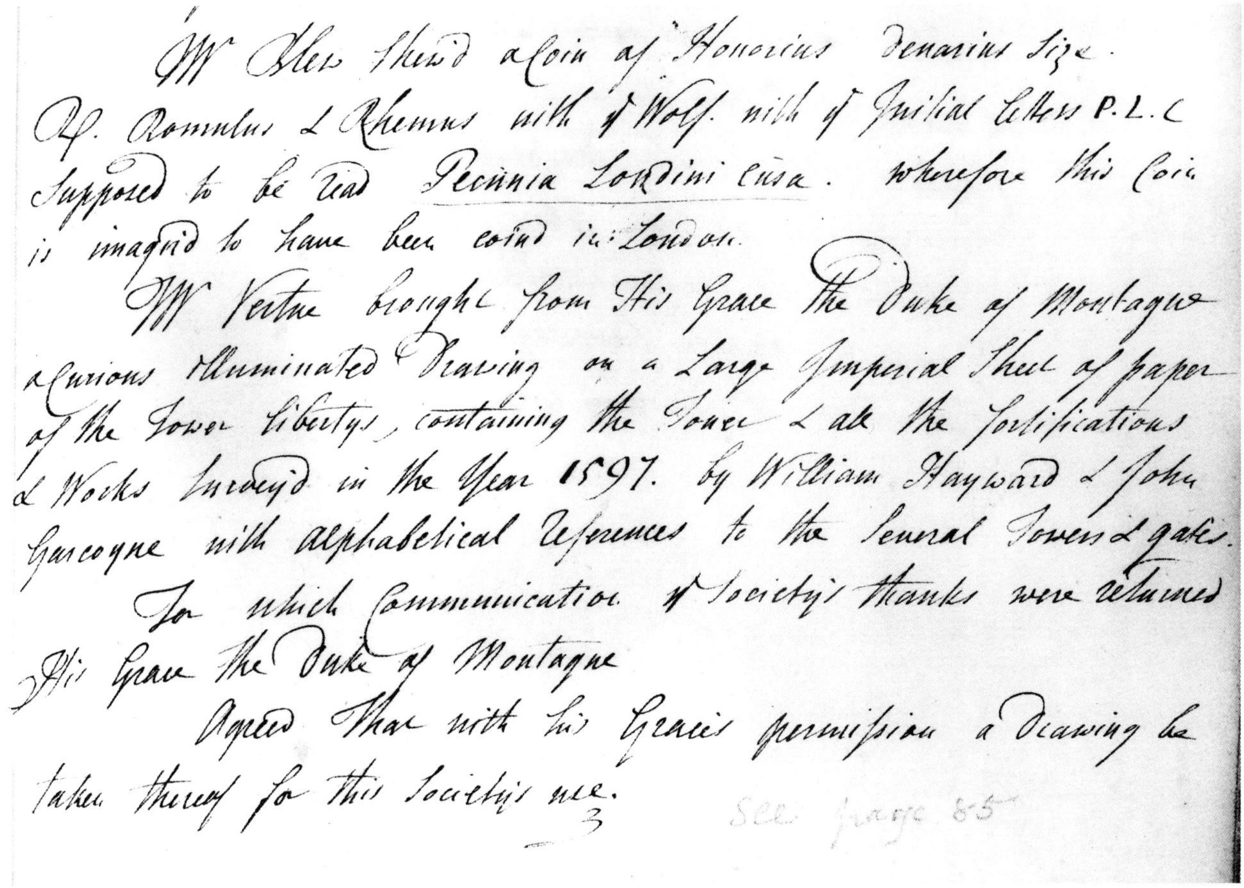

Mr Ames shew'd a Coin of Honorius denarius size.<br>
Rx. Romulus & Rhemus with ye Wolf. with ye Initial Letters P.L.C<br>
Supposed to be read Pecunia Londini Cusa. wherefore this Coin<br>
is imagin'd to have been coin'd in London.<br>
Mr Vertue brought from His Grace the Duke of Montague<br>
a Curious Illuminated Drawing on a Large Imperial Sheet of paper<br>
of the Tower Libertys, containing the Tower & all the fortifications<br>
& Works Surveyd in the Year 1597. by William Hayward & John<br>
Gascoyne with alphabetical References to the Several Towers & gates.<br>
For which Communication ye Society's thanks were returned<br>
His Grace the Duke of Montague<br>
Agreed That with his Graces permission a Drawing be<br>
taken thereof for this Society's use.<br>
3 See page 85

Fig. 2. Description of the original survey of 1597 from volume four of the Society of Antiquaries' minute book.
(The Society of Antiquaries of London)

others, and it would be strange if he had copied the Haiward and Gascoyne plan without indicating his authorship on the drawings. An examination of the handwriting on the Antiquaries' drawing does not reveal it to be Vertue's; indeed, the form of 'y's and 'g's particularly, positively suggest that it is not his work. However, the engraving features writing much more consistent with Vertue's script, and it could well be his work. The absence of his signature on the engraving, which would have sat so comfortably with the compass rose and fleur-de-lys on the left of the plan, makes it impossible to assert confidently that the engraving is by Vertue, but it certainly seems likely.

## The Heath copy

The relationship between the two copies made for the Society of Antiquaries and the plan by Heath in the Public Record Office (Col. Pl. 3) is, however, rather more obscure. As mentioned above, the Heath copy is a pen and ink drawing with colour washes; the left-hand side of the plan is torn and the plan now measures 72.5 cm by 52.5 cm at its greatest extent. Below the title on this plan come the words 'copied May 1741 by *C. Lemprière*', and in the bottom right-hand corner: 'I Heath delin 1752'.[11] Clement Lemprière was a distinguished and experienced draughtsman who was employed by the Ordnance Office in 'Drawing Plans, Profiles &c[a]' from 1715 to the mid-1740s.[12] After the death of Robert Whitehand (of whom more below) in 1724–5 Lemprière was promoted from Assistant Draughtsman to Draughtsman and was put in charge of the Drawing Room at the Tower of London; by 1741 he had a salaried staff of five men working under him.[13] He seems to have continued in office until his death in 1746.[14] By 1752 the number employed 'to Copy and Contract Draughts in the Drawing Room' had risen to fourteen, and among them was one Joseph Heath, second-class draughtsman, and it was he who was responsible for the copy of Lemprière's copy of the Haiward and Gascoyne plan now in the PRO.[15]

Stamped with a broad arrow and among the Ordnance papers in the PRO, this plan seems never to have left the care of the Ordnance Office and its successors. Unfortunately, the Lemprière copy from which it was taken is no longer with these papers, if indeed it ever was.[16] The Heath copy suggests that the Lemprière version was at least as detailed as the drawing in the Antiquaries' library — in fact probably even more so.[17]

Although there are differences in detail between the Heath copy and the Antiquaries' drawing, the two are remarkably similar. The date of May 1741 given for Lemprière's copy indicates that it was made just before the Antiquaries' drawing, for which permission was given on the 28th of that month. However, it seems clear that the two could not have been made entirely independently of one another; the style of presentation of the supporting material on the sides of the plans is virtually identical and typical of eighteenth-century, rather than sixteenth-century plans.

The implication, therefore, is that whoever made the Antiquaries' drawing of the Haiward and Gascoyne plan had Lemprière's copy at their disposal. Unfortunately, the identity of the artist responsible for the Antiquaries' drawing is unknown: the space beneath the title at the top-right corner of the plan, where Lemprière's name is to be found on the Heath version, has been scratched clear of words. The possibility that the Antiquaries' drawing was Lemprière's work, and that it is in fact the missing copy from which Heath worked, is rendered improbable by the presence of many significant details on the Heath plan which are missing from the Antiquaries' drawing, but which can be found on the Whitehand copy (see below).[18]

## The Whitehand copy

The fourth version of the Haiward and Gascoyne plan is also in the Public Record Office, although it spent much of the last century on loan to the Museum of London (Col. Pl. 2). A pen and ink drawing with colour washes, it measures 57.5 cm by 63.5 cm, though the paper on which it is drawn is made up of two, or perhaps even three, sheets stuck together. The box containing the compass rose has been fixed on to the plan and obscures the title of the survey, now written along the top.[19] Although it was recently reproduced in a journal, this copy has gone entirely unremarked upon and its importance has never been recognised.[20] This is perhaps not surprising given that the Public Record Office catalogue describes it as a 'Copy of engraving showing Liberties in 1597', while in fact the plan states that it was taken from the 1597 original by Robert Whitehand in 'January 1712' (Old Style — so what we would now call January 1713).[21]

In January 1713 Robert Whitehand was the Ordnance Office Draughtsman. He had been paid a fixed salary of £100 per year for his work as 'a Draughtsman appointed constantly to attend the Office' since July 1711,[22] though before then he had worked for the Office on at least one commission.[23] Whitehand was in fact the first person to hold a permanent post of this sort at the Ordnance Office — his appointment marked the birth of the Ordnance Drawing Room, which would in time evolve into the Ordnance Survey.[24] Surprisingly little is known about Robert Whitehand: he must have been a very capable draughtsman to be given such a well-paid and skilled job and yet his copy of the Haiward and Gascoyne survey seems to be the only signed Ordnance Office drawing of his to survive. Whitehand continued as Draughtsman during the reign of George I;[25] but his health was clearly faltering by 1724 when he drew up his will. In this, Whitehand left money to one of the Tower labourers, his washerwoman, and instructed his executors to 'deliver all and every my draughts designs sketches Mathematical Instruments and Rulers the severall draughts in fframes and schemes of opticks in my Chamber excepted and excluded to the Surveyor General ... for the use benefit and Improvement of the young persons instructed in the drawing Room in the Tower'.[26] Perhaps this concern with the education of those who were to follow him goes some way to explaining why most of the plans which survive from Whitehand's period of office are the work of his deputy, Lemprière, rather than in his own hand.[27]

Whitehand seems, therefore, to have made his copy of the Haiward and Gascoyne survey within his first two years as the Ordnance Office Draughtsman. Why he made it can only be a matter of speculation; there is certainly no evidence for it being cited in any jurisdictional debates at this time. As a full-time employee of the Office responsible for its plans and drawings, rather than a contractor brought in to execute particular commissions, Whitehand was presumably concerned with the care and condition of the plans already belonging to the Office. It may just have been, therefore, that as Haiward and Gascoyne's original was by this time well over a century old, Whitehand copied it simply

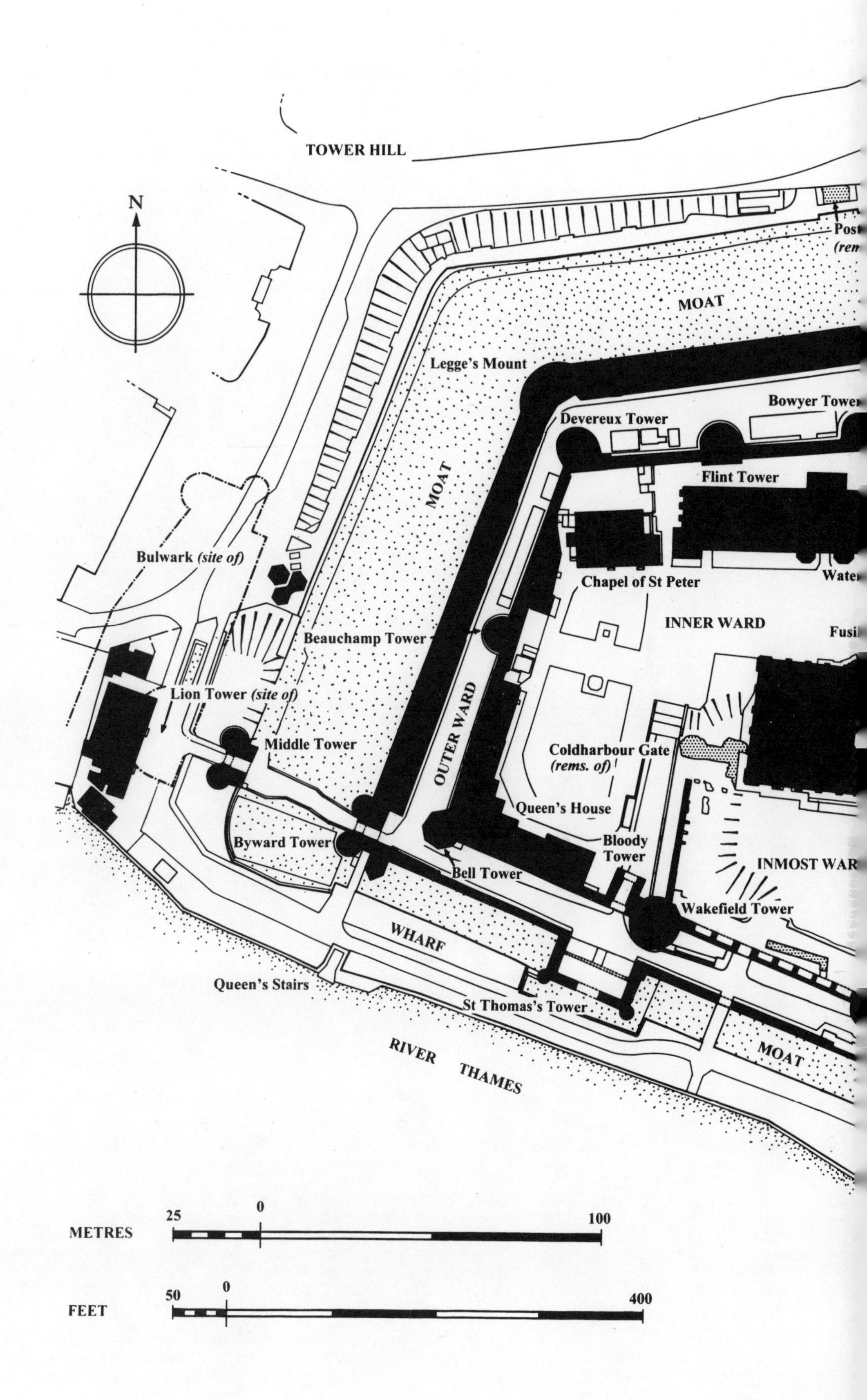


Plan 1. The Tower of London in 2001.
(© Historic Royal Palaces. Drawing by Edward

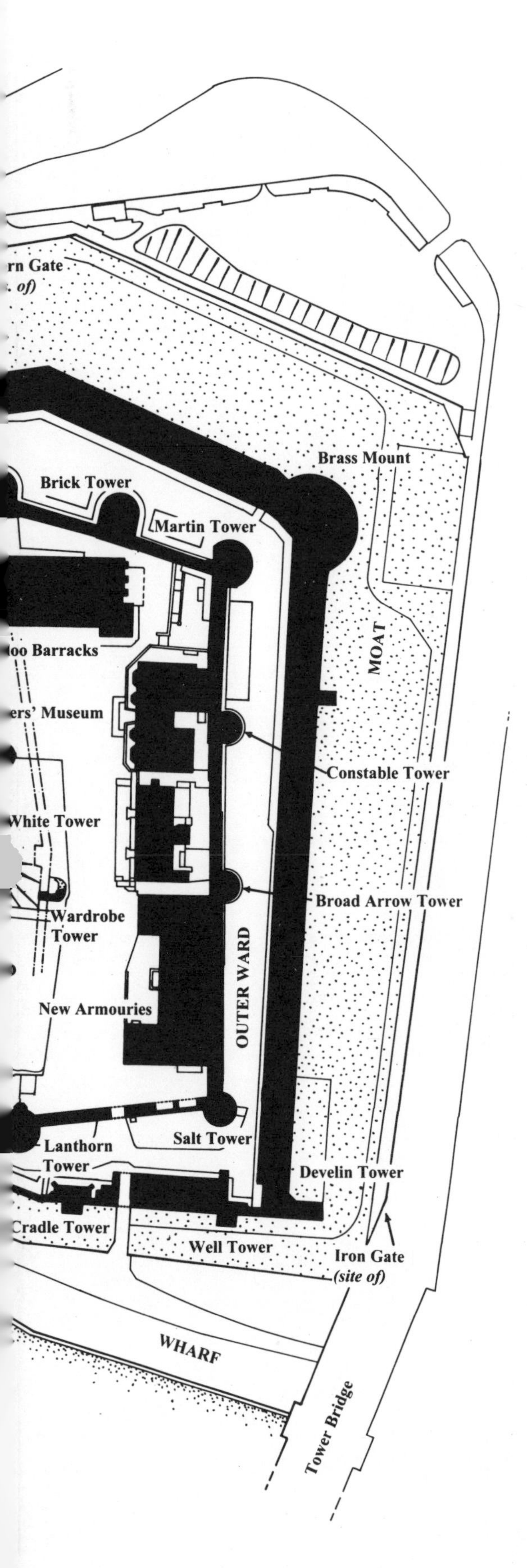


mpey)

EXACT COPY
UGHT of the
IBERTIES.
the year 1597.
IUS HAIWARD
SCOYNE.

undaries of ye Liberties
ears in the Leet Anno

Tower beginning at the
Rams Head in Petty Wales
orth to the end of Tower
to the Mud Wall called
e the Crutched Fryers and
all of London with the Nine
n and above the Broken Tower
og Lane and and so straight
Corner and so on to ye Thames
ner abutting a green line is
iberties.

ent room for Names of pla-
mes of such places are no
to be referr'd to ye Alphabet-
en.

Marks of the
owers.

te.

o the Iron Gate.
Gate.

ver.

Marks for the
the Liberties
ater Gate call'd the
e Mud Wall was call'd
North East of the
e Broken Tower was
Stone corner House.
treet.
the East end of the

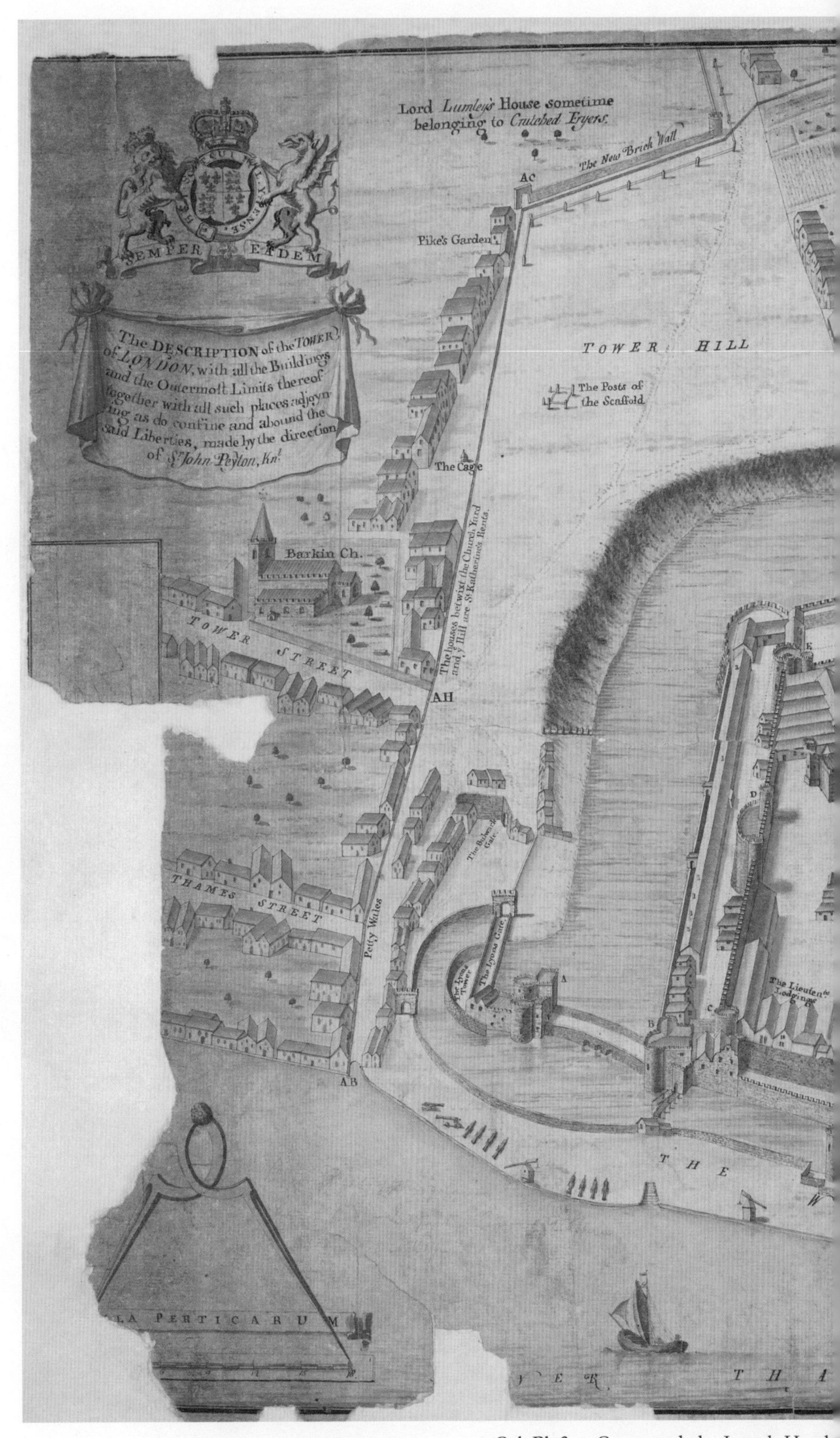


Col. Pl. 3. Copy, made by Joseph Heath
(The

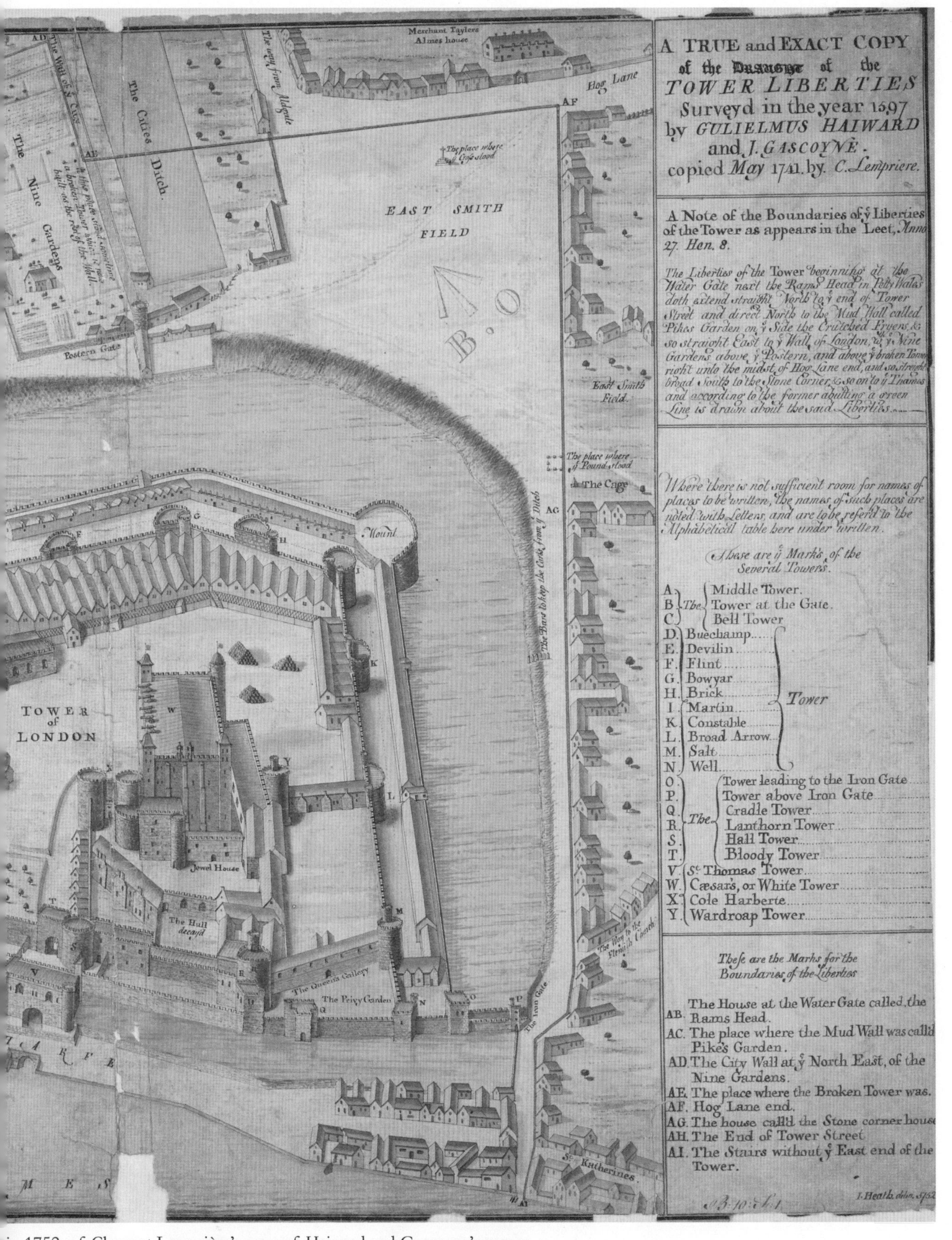


in 1752, of Clement Lemprière's copy of Haiward and Gascoyne's survey.
ublic Record Office (MPH1/214 (2)))

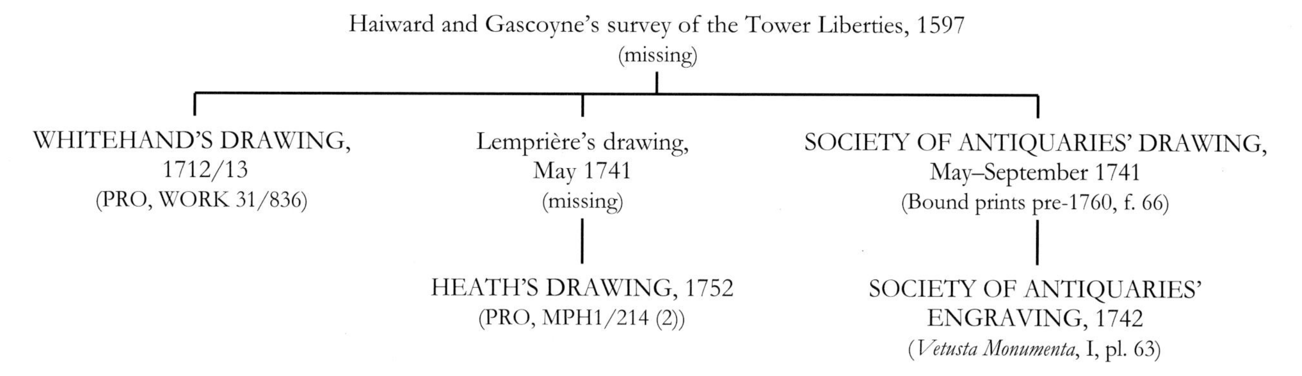


Fig. 3. Diagram showing the relationship of the surviving copies of the 1597 survey to the missing original.

to provide his office with a fresh version, with script in a legible modern hand, to which to refer.[28]

### The relative merits of the copies

The existing copies seem, then, to represent three strains of descent from the original (Fig. 3). As the Society of Antiquaries' engraving is purely a derivative of the Society's drawing, it will be set aside for the time being. The other three, all drawings, are very similar and there is — in particular — very little difference between the way they render the outline of the fortress and the positions of the buildings in and around it.[29] The plans most obviously differ from one another in two ways: their presentation of the supporting text and their attention to the fine details of the buildings they show. While both the Heath drawing and the Society of Antiquaries' drawing show the supporting information in a broad column down the right-hand side of the plan, the Whitehand copy has the same information scattered about the body of the survey in a variety of boxes.[30] As the former is broadly characteristic of eighteenth-century[31] and the latter more of sixteenth-century plans,[32] this suggests that, in this respect, the Whitehand copy is likely to be more faithful to the missing original.[33] The original was apparently larger than any of the surviving copies: Vertue described it as being on a 'large Imperial Sheet of paper' indicating that it was as big as, or even bigger than, the 22 in. by 30 in. of an imperial sheet. All three copies are, however, drawn to the same scale, which was doubtless the scale of Haiward and Gascoyne's own work.[34]

The other aspect in which there is significant difference between the three plans is their attention to the finer details of the buildings shown: an inspection of the way the three record the fenestration of buildings and architectural details such as battlements and chimneys reveals that, in this respect, the Antiquaries' drawing is less sophisticated than the two drawings in the PRO, and that of the PRO drawings, the Whitehand is clearly the more meticulous. A comparison between the way the three versions show the principal window of the Lieutenant's lodgings looking south over the river is one example of this: the Whitehand drawing shows a two-light gothic window with tracery, the Heath drawing represents the window as composed of two lights, but shows no further detail, while the Antiquaries' drawing shows it simply as a large black square, with only the faintest suggestion that it comprised two lights.[35] A similar exercise carried out on many other details of the survey yields broadly the same results.[36]

Therefore, it seems that while the three drawn copies of the 1597 survey are almost identical in outline, in the two main areas of difference there is good reason to think the Whitehand copy is most faithful to the original.[37] Some sense of this is made by what we know of the authorship of the drawings: the Whitehand copy was apparently made directly from the original by a skilled professional draughtsman, the Heath copy — although also the work of a professional — was not taken directly from the original survey and was the work of a less senior draughtsman, while we know nothing of the identity of the artist responsible for the Antiquaries' drawing.

In the absence of the original, then, the 1712/13 copy by Robert Whitehand will be used to explore the origins of the survey and will, for the time being, be assumed to constitute an accurate reproduction of that survey. Unless otherwise specified, references to the Haiward and Gascoyne plan will, from now on, be to the Robert Whitehand copy of the missing original.

## NOTES

[1] *Vetusta Monumenta: quae ad Rerum Britannicarum Memoriam Conservandam Societas Antiquariorum Londini*, 7 vols. (London, 1747-1896), I, plate 63.

[2] Society of Antiquaries of London library, bound volume of prints and drawings before 1760, f.66. As far as I have been able to ascertain this version has only been reproduced in one work on the Tower in the 260 years since it was made: E. Impey and G. Parnell, *The Tower of London* (London, 2000), pp. 48-9.

[3] PRO, MPH1/214 (2).

[4] PRO, WORK 31/836.

[5] In addition to these four copies of the survey, two others may be familiar: the frequently-reproduced coloured version of the engraving of 1742, and the engraving by Henry Mutlow reproduced in J. Bayley, *The History and Antiquities of the Tower of London*, 2 vols. (London, 1825), I, plate II, which seems to have been taken from the 1742 engraving, though reference to the Antiquaries' drawing is made in Bayley's caption.

[6] Society of Antiquaries of London, Minute Book, IV, p. 72. This is the only reference I have found to the first name of 'J' Gascoyne; this piece of information is not recorded on any of the copies and, therefore, indicates both that the Antiquaries were not being shown the 'Whitehand' copy of 1712/13, and that the known copies do not communicate the totality of information contained on the original.

[7] Ibid., p. 85.

[8] Ibid., p. 130.

[9] There are some very minor exceptions, where the engraving shows details omitted by the drawing, such as the windows on the houses near the Bulwark gate.

[10] For George Vertue's engraving of a seventeenth-century plan of Whitehall Palace, which is even more elaborately dressed, see S. Thurley, *The Whitehall Palace Plan of 1670*, London Topographical Society publication 153 (London, 1998).

[11] PRO, MPH1/214 (2).

[12] In 1715 he had drawn up 'Plans Sections and Elevations of the Gun Wharfe, Grand Store house, Cranes &c' at Portsmouth for the Ordnance Office, PRO, WO55/2281, f. 4r. For the history of the Drawing Room at the Tower, see D. W. Marshall, 'Military maps of the eighteenth-century and the Tower of London Drawing Room', *Imago Mundi* 32 (1980), pp. 21-45.

[13] PRO, WO51/102, f. 57v; WO54/199(2); WO54/200, p. 8.

[14] PRO, PROB 11/750, ff. 139v-140r; WO54/207, p. 5.

[15] PRO, WO51/179, f. 48v. I am grateful to Geoffrey Parnell for this reference.

[16] A tantalizing and barely-legible pencil note on the PRO plan reads 'The original of this plan ... Inspector [?] Generals Office 31 ... 1817'; this is perhaps likely to refer to Lemprière's copy rather than to Haiward and Gascoyne's original.

[17] Without Lemprière's copy it is hard to know what to attribute to Heath and what to Lemprière where Heath's plan disagrees with other copies. Heath's omission of the label for 'The Queen's Lodgings' and the window in the eastern tower of the Coldharbour Gate are particularly noticeable. Given the obvious nature of these omissions, and the otherwise extremely careful and detailed nature of the copy, it may well be that these were Heath's, rather than Lemprière's mistakes. The Heath copy includes very few details not found on the other drawn copies, the portcullis in the Bloody Tower is the most notable.

[18] These include the battlements between the Bloody Tower and the Lieutenant's lodgings, the form of the windows on the Ordnance storehouses (the long range of buildings to the north of the White Tower), the windows and chimneys on the Merchant Taylors' almshouse and the labelling of the Roman city wall.

[19] This was presumably attached by Whitehand himself, the text beneath certainly appears to be in the same hand as the title along the top of the sheet.

[20] M. Hutchinson, 'Edward IV's Bulwark: excavations at Tower Hill, London, 1985', *Transactions of the London and Middlesex Archaeological Society*, 47 (1996), pp. 103-44, fig. 5. The caption to this image of the Whitehand copy reads: 'Detail of the Bulwark and the Western Entrance from Haiward & Gascoyne's survey of the Tower in 1597', when in fact the whole of the plan has been reproduced.

[21] To be precise, this is what it *used* to say: the full text of the date is now missing; however, a black and white photograph of the plan survives from its time at the Museum of London and this shows that the full date was 'Ianuary 1712'. The date of the plan is repeated in the obscured text beneath the compass rose, but is now so difficult to read that it is impossible to be certain of the year it records.

[22] Impey and Parnell, *The Tower of London*, p. 70; PRO, WO51/88, f. 121v.

[23] In June 1711 he was paid £30 for 'the Draughts he hath drawne for her Ma^ties^ Service of Port: mahon, Harwich & other places', PRO, WO51/83, f. 55r.

[24] See Impey and Parnell, *The Tower of London*, pp. 69-71; Marshall, 'Military maps of the eighteenth-century and the Tower of London Drawing Room', pp. 21-45; W. A. Seymour, *A History of the Ordnance Survey* (London, 1980).

[25] PRO, WO51/107, f. 124v; WO54/199 (2) and (4). Strangely, the quarterly payments to Whitehand disappear from the Ordnance Bill Books after 1714, however he is included, at the same salary, in the lists of the staff of the office for the rest of his life.

[26] PRO, PROB 11/604, ff. 78r-v. This describes Whitehand as 'of the Tower of London', indicating that at this time he remained a resident of the fortress.

[27] The register of the 'draughts' in the Drawing Room of 1743 records only four plans for which Whitehand was responsible, and all of these were themselves copies of other plans, PRO, WO55/2281, ff. 4r, 29r, 45r.

[28] It makes sense for Whitehand to have made this copy of an existing plan in the middle of winter, which must have been an inhospitable time to survey buildings for new plans.

[29] None of the three copies is utterly identical to another in outline, but they are extraordinarily similar and differ from one another in such essentials as the angles of the

curtain walls and the line of the Liberty by less than a single degree in almost every case.

[30] That the original did indeed contain such supplementary information is also shown by the Society of Antiquaries' minute book which specifically describes the 1597 survey as having 'Alphabetical references'.

[31] For example, the battle plans at Boughton described by Nicholas Barker in Tessa Murdoch (ed.), *Boughton House: The English Versailles* (London, 1992), pp. 170-3.

[32] See, for example, P. D. A. Harvey, *Maps in Tudor England* (London, 1993), figs. 8, 14, 27, 32, 42, 44, 52, 58, 59, 62, 63, 78, 80, 81.

[33] It is also noticeable that the Heath and Antiquaries' copies show a larger area than the Whitehand. However, that the original was probably the proportions of Whitehand's copy is indicated by the fact that no more buildings are shown on the larger 1741 copies; instead, where the area shown has been extended westwards, to allow for more prominent royal arms, an oblong box has been inserted to obscure the absence of information on the original about the streets further west, whereas houses shown on the eastern section of the Whitehand version have been covered on the others by the inclusion of the panel of text.

[34] The scale was about 1:800. I am very grateful to Edward Impey for working this out.

[35] That the window was actually as the Whitehand drawing shows rather than as the Antiquaries' drawing shows it is, in this case, indicated by Hollar's mid-seventeenth-century drawing of the area (Fig. 9).

[36] For example, Whitehand shows tracery in the windows of the hall, the Chapel of St Peter, and 'Barkin Church', the way the tower to the south of the Lanthorn Tower curves round the Lanthorn, the decorative pinnacles to the gables of the 'Queen's Lodgings' and the battlements which run down the east side of the building of the 'Queen's Lodgings'.

[37] The spelling of the words on the plan are also more antiquated on the Whitehand copy than on the other two versions: for example where the 1741 copies have 'Privy' garden and 'Lord Lumley's House sometime belonging to Crutched Fryers', Whitehand has the 'Pryvy' garden, 'Lord Lumblies' and 'Crotchet Fryers'. On the whole it is only in form of spelling that the three versions differ in terms of the text they include, though in the title beneath the royal arms Whitehand renders as 'ye Buylding & ye outermost liuings' what the 1741 copies have as 'Buildings and the Outermost Limits'; this is probably more an indication of how unfamiliar and difficult to decipher Elizabethan hands had become by the early eighteenth century than anything else.

# II. THE ORIGINS OF THE SURVEY

## Introduction

ONE of the things which makes the Haiward and Gascoyne survey so fascinating is the wealth of supporting information which it includes, both crammed into boxes in blank areas and intermingled with the landscape and buildings themselves. As befits a 'draught of the TOWER LIBERTIES', much of this text relates directly to the delineation of the Liberty of the Tower, that is, the area immediately surrounding the castle, comprising Tower Hill, East Smithfield and the wharf, over which the Tower (as the instrument of the sovereign) claimed to have direct and sole jurisdiction, and the inhabitants of which enjoyed special privileges and immunities. The descriptive title of the survey (in the box below the royal arms) and the text of the 1536 court leet pronouncement, as well as the description of the turning points of the boundary line at the bottom of the alphabetical key on the right-hand side, all refer directly to the Liberty of the Tower. Every indication is that the purpose of the survey was to show the position of the boundary in a way that left no room for equivocation. Yet the plan also contains an enormous amount of information incidental to the position of the boundary of the Liberty, not least in its detailed depiction of dozens of buildings within the walls of the fortress. In order to understand why such a survey was commissioned, it is necessary to look more closely at the contemporary status of the boundary and the controversies in which it was embroiled.

## The Tower Liberties in the late sixteenth century

Disputes about the boundary of the Liberty of the Tower — the point at which royal and civic authority met — were older than most of the buildings themselves,[38] and attempts to fix that boundary were being made as early as 1214–15.[39] The question of jurisdiction was far from settled by the mid-sixteenth century as can be seen from the 1536 court leet pronouncement on the exact limits of the Liberty cited in the box of text on Tower Hill on the Haiward and Gascoyne survey.[40] Simon Thurley has suggested that this proclamation may have been part of a more general assertion of royal authority in the capital in the mid-1530s masterminded by Thomas Cromwell. As he has shown, a similar initiative can certainly be seen in the Act of 1536 which made quite clear the pre-eminence of royal authority in the environs of Whitehall.[41] However, as the original court leet records seem to have disappeared, it is difficult to ascertain the extent to which the verdicts of that body were the direct embodiment of a royal or Cromwellian initiative rather than the product of a genuinely local assembly.

Whatever the genesis of the court leet judgement of 1536, the verdict was clearly insufficient to resolve the debate about the status of the immediate environs of the Tower of London. Another attempt was made to settle the issue in 1570 when a series of 'presentments' were issued which set out the extent of the Tower's jurisdiction.[42] The line defined by the 'presentments' was virtually identical to that declared by the Henrician court leet (and later shown in the Haiward and Gascoyne plan). Unfortunately, this very precise ruling on the Liberty seems to have been made by a committee which not only lacked an impartial senior judge but which was, instead, composed of Tower officials. Not surprisingly, therefore, the 'presentments' seem to have been entirely ignored by the Lord Mayor.

Although the position of the boundary which separated them was only one of the many areas of dispute between the Tower and the City in the course of Elizabeth I's reign, the uncertainty in which it was shrouded lay at the heart of almost all of them. On 17 March 1579 the Privy Council had asked the Master of the Rolls and the Master of the Court of Requests to carry out an official enquiry into the dispute then raging between the Gentleman Porter of the Tower[43] and the Lord Mayor.[44] This commission did not report in full until October 1585 and even then ruled only on the privileges allowed to Tower employees and not on the physical extent of the Tower's control.[45] Without resolution of the crucial question of jurisdiction little was actually solved, and six years later the Lord Mayor started petitioning members of the Privy Council to 'grant a commission for the hearing and determining of the matters in dispute between the City and the Tower of London, touching the bounds and Liberties of both places'.[46] The calls for official consideration of the status of the Liberties were to be repeated for six more years before any action was taken.[47]

That the disputes, in the volatile and occasionally explosive atmosphere of London in the mid-1590s, were more than academic squabbling is demonstrated by the events of 29 June 1595.[48] On this day, in an incident which has been seen as the culmination of a series of disorders in the capital over the preceding decade, a crowd of City apprentices rioted on Tower Hill. When the Lord Mayor marched in with his sword aloft — thus declaring his authority — to disperse the crowd, instead of being aided by Tower officials, 'he was, by divers of the warders and others belonging to the Tower ... in a very formidable manner told, that his sword ought not in that place to be carried erect'.[49] The riot was not, of course, actually initiated by a row over the position of the boundary of the Tower Liberties, but showed that the issue was sufficiently emotive for the Lieutenant and his men to concern themselves more with the infringement of the Liberty by the Mayor than with quelling a rioting crowd of perhaps 1,000 men just outside the walls of the Tower.

The investigation which followed the riot of June 1595 contributed further to the mood of uncertainty in London, revealing, as it did, that the Lieutenant of the Tower, Sir Michael Blount, had been involved in a conspiracy to hold the Tower against the Privy Council on the death of Elizabeth I.[50] Calls for the Liberty issue to be resolved continued and it seems as though the events of 1595 encouraged the Privy Council to take more heed of them.[51] In September 1596 the City was assembling its most learned men to consider 'what manner of Comissyon and in what forme is fitt to be procured for the limiting of the boundes betweene this Cittie and y^e^ Tower of london'.[52]

A year was still to pass before the commissioners were appointed and the Privy Council was determined during that time to prevent any further clashes; in January 1597, with the prospect of the inauguration of a new Mayor, the Privy Council wrote to the Lieutenant of the Tower, Sir Richard Berkley, to impress on him his duty to ensure that a 'quiet and peaceable course be observed'.[53] The question of how far the Mayor could walk with his sword before him was made no simpler by the fact that the boundary stones which had once delineated the Liberty had been moved; the Council, therefore, charged the Lieutenant and the 'chiefe of the city ... to gouverne the matter so as no disorder be comitted nor wronge done to the liberties either the one part or th'other ...'.[54]

This atmosphere of trust was short-lived: on 4 May 1597 the Council sent a message to the Lieutenant and Gentleman Porter of the Tower 'requiring them to forbeare at this tyme the perambulacion or procession that the[y] usually make on Ascension Daie about the circuits and limittes of the Tower, because of the controversie at this present betwixt the citty and the Tower touchinge the said limites'. This time the Council clearly did not feel that the Lieutenant and Mayor were sufficiently conciliatory to prevent rituals in which the boundary featured from becoming a brawl. It appears that something had happened at the last moment to necessitate the cancellation of the perambulation, a telling postscript to the Privy Council record reads: 'Entred thus briefly because it was to be dispatched away in haste'.[55]

### John Peyton and the Tower Liberties

So it seems that in the spring of 1597, the year in which Haiward and Gascoyne executed their survey, the debate over ownership of the Liberty was more controversial and explosive than ever. In June 1597 Sir John Peyton (1544–1630), by whose 'direction' the survey declares itself to have been made, was appointed Lieutenant of the Tower.[56] Better known for his subsequent governorship of Jersey (1603–30), Peyton had been a colonel in the forces defending the Queen's person during the Armada scare of 1588, had held the receivership of Norfolk and Huntingdon since 1593 and was Deputy Lieutenant of Cambridgeshire.[57] Given the date of the Haiward and Gascoyne plan (1597) and the fact that Peyton was not appointed until June of that year, the survey must have been initiated within the first few months of his tenure. Things did not start well for Peyton, he was incapacitated by an illness in the summer of 1597 and then, in October, John Gerard and John Arden escaped from his custody.[58] The office of Lieutenant was undoubtedly a difficult one: since Sir Michael Blount had been deprived of his post in November 1595 two other men had been appointed Lieutenant but neither had lasted more than a year.[59] Peyton was to continue as Lieutenant until July 1603 when James I granted his request to be relieved of a post which Peyton himself described as 'only composed of trouble, danger, charge and vexation'; he was appointed, instead, Governor of Jersey.[60]

Little evidence, beyond the plan itself, has been found of Haiward and Gascoyne's original commission; however, a very telling paper compiled by Peyton while the plan was being made does shed some light on the issue. Entitled 'A declaracon of

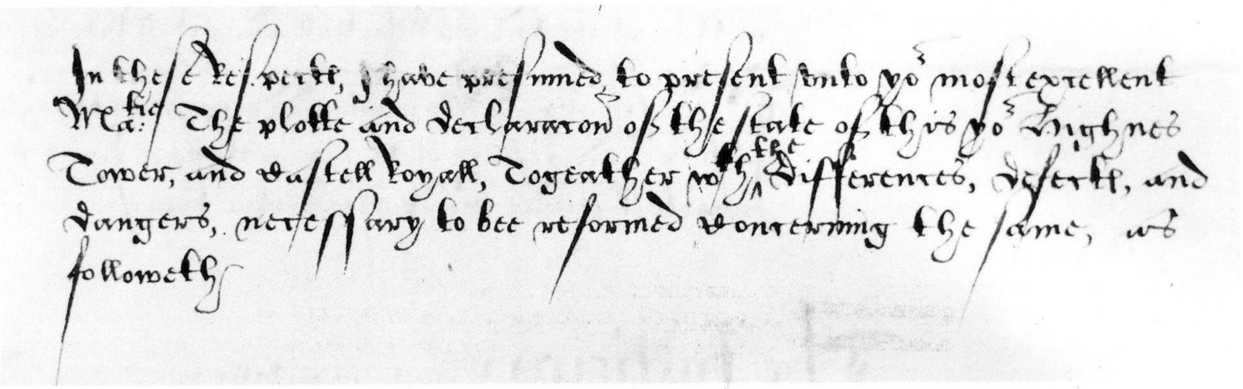
In these Respectes, I have presumed to present unto yo$^{r}$ most excellent Ma:$^{tie}$ The plotte and declaracon of the state of this yo$^{r}$ Highnes Tower, and Castell Royall, Togeather w$^{th}$ the differences, defectes, and dangers, necessary to bee reformed concerning the same, as followeth

Fig. 4. The one contemporary reference to the 'plotte' of the Tower of London, from Sir John Peyton's 1597 report on the state of the castle.
(© The Board of Trustees of the Armouries (RA, MS I. 243))

the state of yo$^{r}$ Highnes Tower of London', the document survives in three largely similar forms: a formal draft of October 1597 (Appendix A),[61] a second version also of that year comprising the text of the first version but with substantial annotations and additions in the margins,[62] and a completed version incorporating those additions dated September 1598 (Appendix B).[63]

The document comprises two principal sections: first is the 'declaracon' of the state of the Tower itself, which literally sets out what the Tower contained and what the duties of the Lieutenant were as governor of the castle, concluding with Peyton's undertaking to try and carry out those duties. The first of the duties which Peyton ascribes to his job was to establish the condition of the fortress and whether it was 'weakened, by decayes, disorders, or other defects', while his other duties were to be to 'governe and commaund the guarde', to oversee and keep the peace between inhabitants and officers of the Tower, and to interrogate prisoners. The second part of the document is a detailed report on the condition of the fortress addressed to the Queen which catalogues 'Differences Necessary to bee decyded', 'Defectes, Needfull to bee be supplyed' and 'Disorders Meete to be Reformed'. The first of the 'Differences Necessary to bee decyded' was that the 'cittye of London did and doth pretend Title, unto y[ou]r Ma:$^{ties}$ soyle of Tower hill, (and Eastsmithfield) even unto the ditch of the Tower'. In this section Peyton explained the importance of asserting royal jurisdiction over Tower Hill and urged the Queen not to 'suffer this pretended Intrusion and incroachment'.[64]

In the earlier versions of the document, Peyton included a paragraph between the two parts which spells out the fact that the second half represents a fulfilment of some of the duties outlined in the first. This reads 'In these Respectes, I have presumed to present unto yo$^{r}$ most excellent Ma:$^{tie}$ The plotte and declaracon of the state of this yo$^{r}$ Highnes Tower, and Castell Royal, Togeather w$^{th}$ the differences, defects, and dangers, necessary to bee reformed concerning the same, as followeth' (Fig. 4). The reference here to the 'plotte' which Peyton was clearly intending to present to the Queen with the written document must surely be to the plan being made by Haiward and Gascoyne specifically for Peyton in the course of that year. However, this crucial paragraph, containing the only reference to the 'plotte', is crossed out in the second version of the manuscript of the same year and omitted altogether from the final version.

The strange absence of any mention of the 'plotte' from the later versions of the 'declaracon' is compounded by the fact that this plan, originally to have been presented to the Queen with the 'declaracon', was described as being of the 'Tower, and Castell Royall' rather than of the Tower and Liberties.[65] Not only is this suggested by the wording of the paragraph in which it is referred to, but its existence is specifically mentioned in tandem with the 'declaracon' of the nature of the Lieutenant's charge and responsibilities, rather than in the section of the document relating to the dispute over the Liberties. The Haiward and Gascoyne plan as we know it is partly, if not principally, concerned with the line of the Liberty, yet there is nothing in the first version of the 'declaracon' to confirm that this was the subject of the 'plotte' which was to accompany it.

It is here suggested that both the omission of any mention of the 'plotte' from the later drafts of the 'declaracon' and the inconsistency between the description of that 'plotte' in the early draft and the Haiward and Gascoyne plan as it survives were due to a change in the purpose of the plan in the later months of 1597.

In the second and third versions of the 'declaracon', at the end of the section detailing the first of the 'Differences' which needed resolution — the establishment of royal control over the Tower Liberties — an extra paragraph is inserted which is not included in the first draft. This, which was to be in a different, 'romayne', script reads: 'For decidinge of this antient and inconvenient controversy touchinge the Tower liberties and priveleges, your Ma$^{tie}$ hath graunted a comission to the Judges, unto whome I have delivered apparant proofes for your Highnes title'.[66] This was the commission for which the Lord Mayor had been pressing since 1591, and which had finally been appointed by 4 October 1597 when the City sent its representatives to attend on the commissioners.[67] The first version of the 'declaracon', dated October 1597, was perhaps, therefore, compiled before the commission had been appointed, but these circumstances had obviously changed by the time the second version was made in the final months of the year. Peyton had clearly been involved in giving evidence to the commission and doubtless had had ample opportunity to give his opinion on this matter directly. Crucially, however, Peyton provided the commissioners with more than just his opinion: in his own words it was these commissioners 'unto whome I have delivered apparent proofes for your Highnes titles'.

The question is of what did these proofs consist? Certainly chapter-and-verse corroboration was something by which Peyton seems to have set particular store. Later in the same document Peyton describes the severe shortage of watchmen to guard the Tower, and points out that 'Yo$^{r}$ Ma$^{tie}$ hath in paye divers officers & arteficers ... w$^{ch}$ ought to watch and warde in the Tower'. There follows a one-line paragraph which asserts that this obligation was 'Proved by establishment 25$^{o}$ Julii An$^{o}$.1 H.8.'. Peyton goes on to quote an incident of 'the xx$^{th}$ of October An$^{o}$3.H.8.', which is again followed by a one-line paragraph, here reading 'Proved by the order signed by the said S$^{r}$ Thos: Seymor'. Peyton was conscientious in his consideration of these problems and was meticulous too in his use of named and quoted historical precedents to support his suggestions, all of which must have necessitated extensive research. It is also interesting to note his particular use of Henrician precedents as his 'proofes', it may be that these shared some of the considerable authority attached to that well-remembered monarch.

The one document commissioned by Peyton which names and quotes a Henrician precedent to prove the line of the Tower Liberties is — of course — the Haiward and Gascoyne plan,[68] and in this light it is suggested that the proof Peyton provided to the commission investigating the Liberties question consisted partly or entirely of the Haiward and Gascoyne survey.

If a plan, intended at first to accompany Peyton's 'declaracon', was instead submitted to the commission considering the status of the Liberties, the subsequent disappearance of reference to it from the text of the 'declaracon' would be explained. This suggested change in the use of the plan would also explain why such prominence is given to the line of the Liberty in its final form, something not implied by the description of the 'plotte' in the first draft of the 'declaracon'. This hypothesis would also make some sense of one of the great enigmas of the plan as it survives: the inclusion of details of so many buildings within the walls of the Tower on a plan of the Liberties.[69] If the original survey was to have accompanied a description of the nature of the Lieutenant's responsibilities as guardian of the Tower of London, it would be entirely appropriate for the plan to have included details of its buildings, among them the Lieutenant's own house and the sovereign's lodgings.[70] But if, in the course of its preparation, the function of the survey altered and it was to be submitted instead to a commission considering the position and status of the Liberties, the rest of the plan could have been completed with an eye to the line of that Liberty. It may even be that the plan was completed before a decision was taken to submit it to the Liberties commission, and that only the title, and some of the text relating to the line of the Liberty, was added to make it suitable for this purpose.[71]

In the absence of further evidence, only speculation is possible. However, it is suggested here that this posited change in function would go a long way to explaining the inclusion, on a plan containing such a mass of information about the Liberty, of a detailed delineation of the buildings within the Tower itself; and is consistent with the presence and then absence of mention of a 'plotte' of the Tower in Peyton's 'declaracon' of 1597/8.

## The surveyors

If the survey was made for the Lieutenant of the Tower, in part to substantiate a claim regarding the

Fig. 5. Map of Longham in Norfolk by William Haiward.
(Reproduced by permission of the Earl of Leicester and the Trustees of Holkham Estate)

status of the Liberty, it might make some sense of the way in which it seems to have been commissioned. William Haiward was a successful and skilled land surveyor from East Anglia, who carried out numerous surveys of estates and land holdings in and around King's Lynn and the north of Norfolk in the late sixteenth and early seventeenth centuries.[72] In his long career, from 1591 to the 1630s, he seems to have worked on only three projects outside this area, the second of which was the 1597 plan of the Tower of London.[73]

John Peyton and William Haiward came from the same part of eastern England and it seems highly probable that, if they did not know one another personally, they were aware of each other professionally.[74] A document of 1583, held among the papers of Sir Edward Coke who purchased a portion of his Norfolk lands from Sir John Peyton, describes one Henry Haiward as the executor of one John Peyton.[75] The relationship of these men to the Haiward and Peyton of the 1597 plan is unclear, but it may well be that the two families were used to dealing with one another in county affairs. In 1605 Sir John Peyton was one of those who joined Chief Justice Sir John Popham in an initiative to drain some areas of fenland for which

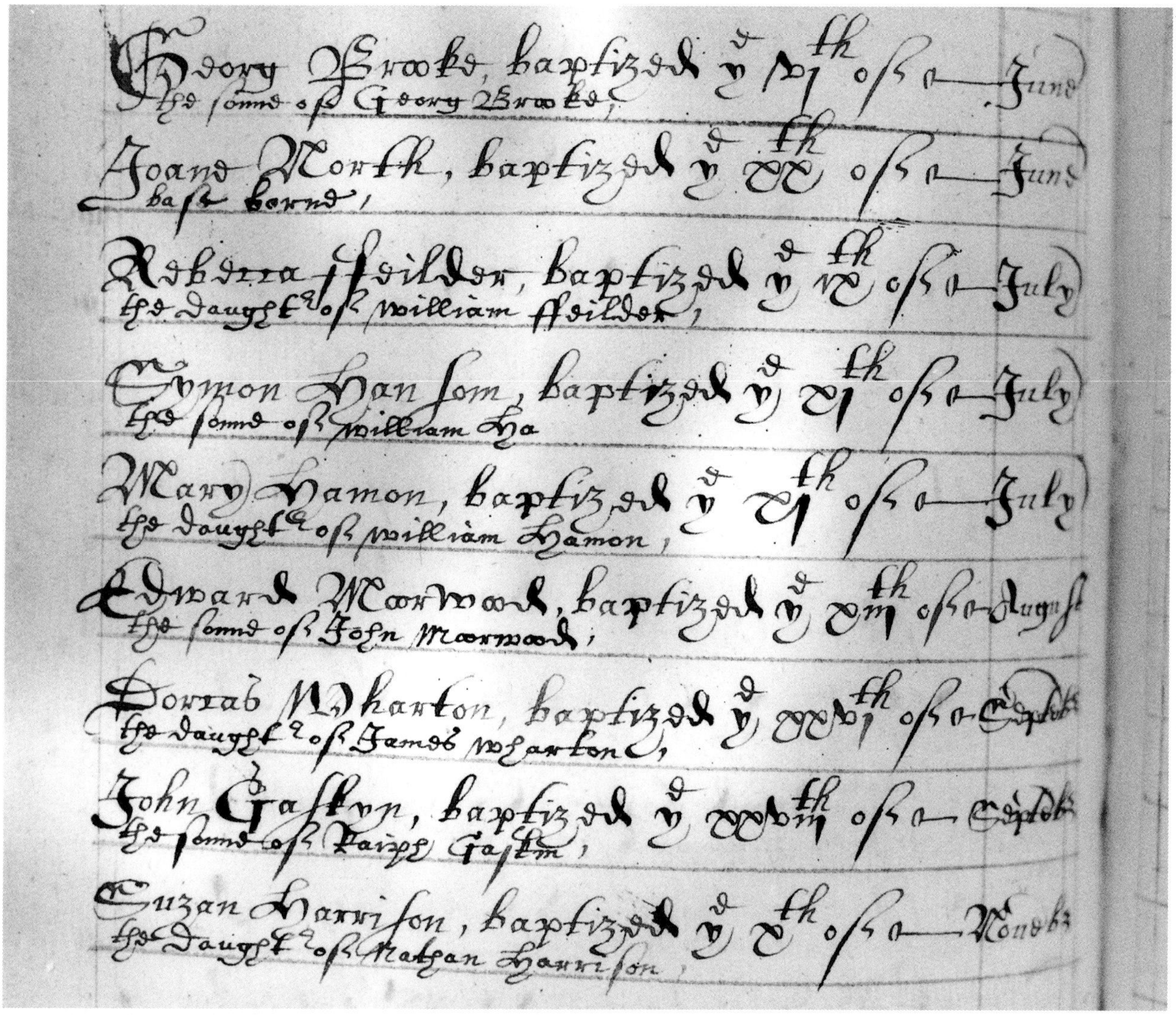
George Brooke, baptized ye vjth of June
the sonne of George Brooke,
Joane North, baptized ye xth of June
base borne,
Rebecca ffielder, baptized ye xth of July
the daughter of william ffielder,
Symon Hansom, baptized ye vjth of July
the sonne of william Ha
Mary Hamon, baptized ye vjth of July
the daughter of william Hamon,
Edward Marwood, baptized ye xvjth of August
the sonne of John Marwood;
Dorcas Wharton, baptized ye xxvjth of Septemb
the daughter of James Wharton,
John Gaskyn, baptized ye xxviijth of Septemb
the sonne of Raiphe Gaskin,
Suzan Harrison, baptized ye vth of Novemb
the daughter of Nathan Harrison,

Fig. 6. Register of the Chapel of St Peter ad Vincula in the Tower of London. Among those baptized in 1596 was one of the many children of Raiph Gasquoine or Gaskin. (© Historic Royal Palaces)

William Haiward appears to have made both a written and a drawn survey. Indeed, one of the only two surviving versions of that important drawn survey derives from a copy made for the Peyton family.[76] It seems likely that Peyton recruited the experienced land surveyor William Haiward from his own county of Norfolk to undertake a survey of the Tower of London. The 1597 plan was not made for the Ordnance Office, which even in 1597 must have had able draughtsmen and land surveyors in its employ,[77] but specifically for Sir John Peyton himself, making it even more probable that he would have approached a surveyor known to him personally. Haiward seems to have left London soon after the completion of the survey and in 1598 was undertaking a survey of Great Wavering. He does not appear to have worked in London again.

William Haiward's draughtsmanship is characterized by remarkable sophistication and attention to detail combined with a strong aesthetic sense. The undated map of Longham which survives at Holkham Hall (Fig. 5) displays these traits.[78] Brightly coloured with gold, green, red and yellow, decorated with an elaborate strapwork cartouche and dividers, and meticulously indexed in the margins, it gives a sense of what the original 'illuminated drawing' with which George Vertue so interested the Antiquaries might have looked like.

While William Haiward's surveys survive in some number, the work of John Gascoyne does not appear to have endured and nothing is known of him.[79] The equal accreditation given to William Haiward and John Gascoyne on the 1597 survey would suggest that the latter was no mere assistant, but intimately involved in either the surveying or draughting of the plan. Given that Haiward had apparently not worked in London before and that the two men seem never to have worked together again, it may well be that Gascoyne was local to London and able to bring specifically urban surveying experience to bear on the project.[80] In this context it is interesting to note how often the unusual name 'Gascoyne' appears in the register of the Chapel of St Peter ad Vincula of the Tower of London in the 1590s (Fig. 6). Between 1587 and 1596 the baptism of seven children of one 'Raiph Gasquoine', who was perhaps the 'Maist[r] Gascoigne [a] ward[e]r' buried in the chapel on 28 August 1609, are recorded in the register.[81] Whether John Gascoyne, the surveyor, was part of this family is impossible to say, but the absence of information about this man should not cloud the fact that the survey was quite likely as much his work as Haiward's.[82]

## NOTES

[38] For more on the history of the dispute over Tower Hill see V. D. Lipman, 'The jurisdiction of the Tower authorities outside the walls', in J. Charlton (ed.), *The Tower of London: its Buildings and Institutions* (London, 1978), pp. 144-53; and the unpublished report by Stephen Priestley for Historic Royal Palaces, 1997/8.

[39] 'In 1214-15 £12 were spent on building a mud wall between the Tower and the City — presumably as an outer boundary rather than as a defensible barrier'; H. Colvin (ed.), *The History of the King's Works,* 6 vols. (London, 1962-82), II, p. 710.

[40] Also quoted in Corporation of London Record Office (hereafter CLRO), Misc. MSS 171/1, 'A Brief Note or Abstract of the Proofs on the part of her Matie touching the differences between her Highness and the Mayor and Commonalty of the City of London'.

[41] S. Thurley, 'Whitehall Palace and Westminster 1400-1600: a royal seat in transition', in D. Gaimster and P. Stamper (eds.), *The Age of Transition: The Archaeology of English Culture 1400-1600* (Oxford, 1997), pp. 101-2.

[42] BL, Add. MS 14044, ff. 38r-41v; CLRO, Misc. MSS 171/1 'Anno 1570: Presentments by the Queens Majesties Inquest of the Tower of London'; PRO, WO55/1776, ff. 54v-55r.

[43] Gentleman Porter, though officially answerable to the Lieutenant of the Tower, seems to have been a position which in reality allowed considerable independence; indeed several Gentlemen Porters appear to have taken active advantage of the jurisdiction disputes between the City and Tower, building and letting houses in the Liberty for personal profit, see, for example: *Analytical Index to the series of Records known as the Remembrancia* (London, 1878), pp. 426-8; CLRO, Rep. 22, f. 161r. For a contemporary record of his and the Lieutenant's oaths see BL, Add. MS 14044, ff. 2r-v.

[44] *Remembrancia*, p. 428.

[45] CLRO, Rep. 21, f. 106v; Jour. 21, ff. 472r-v.

[46] *Remembrancia*, pp. 553-4.

[47] CLRO, Rep. 22, f. 315v; Rep. 23, ff. 545r, 593r; *Remembrancia*, p. 237.

[48] For the 'crisis' in the capital at this time see I. W. Archer, *The Pursuit of Stability: Social Relations in Elizabethan London* (Cambridge, 1991).

[49] W. Maitland, *The History of London*, 2 vols. (London, 1756), I, p. 278; John Stow, *The Abridgement of the English Chronicle ... continued ... by E*[dmond] *H*[owe] (London, 1611), p. 394.

[50] Roger B. Manning, 'The prosecution of Sir Michael Blount, Lieutenant of the Tower of London, 1595', *Bulletin of the Institute of Historical Research* LVII (1984), pp. 216-24; CLRO, Rep. 23, f. 414r; R. Lemon and M. A. Everett Green (eds.), *Calendar of State Papers, Domestic Series, of the Reign of Elizabeth* (hereafer *CSPD*), 5 vols. (London 1865-70), 1595-7, pp. 82, 137.

[51] CLRO, Rep. 23, f. 545r.

[52] CLRO, Rep. 23, f. 580v.

[53] J. R. Dasent (ed.), *Acts of the Privy Council of England* (hereafter *APC*), 32 vols. (London, 1890-1907), XXVI, p. 413.

[54] '... the said bowndes of which ... there be no certaintie because the markes are said to be chaunged which should distinguish them ...', ibid.; also see *Remembrancia*, p. 433 for the Mayor demanding that the Lieutenant of the Tower replace the boundary stone which he had removed.

[55] *APC*, XXVII, p. 86.

[56] S. Williams (ed.), *Letters Written by John Chamberlain during the Reign of Queen Elizabeth*, Camden Society 79 (London, 1869), p. 4; *Historical Manuscripts Commission: Calendar of the Manuscripts of the Marquess of Salisbury at Hatfield House*, 24 vols. (London, 1883-1976), VII, p. 248.

[57] *CSPD*, 1596, p. 434; 1595-7, p. 269. For Peyton's activities in East Anglia in the 1580s and 1590s, see A. Hassell Smith and G. M. Baker (eds.), *The Papers of Nathaniel Bacon of Stiffkey*, 3 vols. (Norwich, 1979-90), II, pp. 27-9; III, pp. 7, 68-9, 247, 284, 291-2, 305-7, 317, 367-8.

[58] *HMC Salisbury*, VII, pp. 417-18.

[59] They were Sir Drue Drury, from 1595 to 1596, and Sir Richard Berkley, from 1596 to 1597. The Catholic priest, John Gerard, who had been imprisoned in the Tower dur-

ing Berkley's tenure there remarked: 'I believe he [Berkley] was moved out of compassion, for some time after my escape a gentleman of position told me that he had heard Sir Richard Berkeley, this same Lieutenant, say that he had freely resigned his office, because he no longer wished to be an instrument in such torture of innocent men.' *John Gerard: the Autobiography of an Elizabethan*, trans. Philip Caraman (London, 1951), p. 112.

[60] 'a place of all others best agreeing with my desires', *HMC Salisbury*, XV, pp. 174, 209-10; BL, Add. MS 6177, f. 128r. If Peyton was exhausted by the demands of his post by 1603 it is perhaps not surprising: during his tenure the Tower had seen the capture and execution of the Earl of Essex, the imprisonment of the Earl of Desmond, the accession of James I and the first period of royal residence at the fortress for over forty years, and the imprisonment and attempted suicide of Sir Walter Ralegh.

[61] Royal Armouries, MS I. 243.

[62] Somerset Record Office, DD/MI Box 18/43.

[63] Bodleian Library, MS Eng Hist e 195.

[64] These quotations are from the October 1597 version of the 'declaracon', see Appendix A for a transcription.

[65] In the Somerset Record Office version of the 'declaracon', parentheses have been inserted into this sentence which imply this even more; reading 'The Plott (and declaracon of the State) of this yor Highnes Tower and Castell Royal'.

[66] The following quotations are from the October 1598 version of the survey, see Appendix B for a transcription.

[67] 'Item yt is ordred yt Sr Willm Webb knight mr Recorder Mr Garrard Aldran undr Chamblin shall repaire to the two LLs Chiefe Justice and chiefe Baron and others the Judges in Commission for determyning ye Controversies towchinge the lymittes and boundes betweene this Cittie and the Lieutennte of ye Tower'; CLRO, Rep. 24, f. 130v.

[68] Perhaps in this case, again, Peyton unearthed the text of a Henrician precedent, the court leet verdict of 1536. There were extant official descriptions of the extent of the Tower Liberties made during the reign of Queen Elizabeth, but these were passed over in favour of a precedent of 1536, although the line described was the same. In this instance, Peyton illustrated on the survey precisely the line of that boundary, and where place names had changed since 1536, gave both.

[69] That the 'plotte' mentioned in the first version of Peyton's 'declaracon' was to relate to the first part of that document, which considered the responsibilities of the Lieutenant, rather than to illustrate the defects mentioned in the second part is further strongly suggested by the absence of any specific illustrations of any of these 'defects' on the finished plan.

[70] It is also entirely consistent with this interpretation that labels for many buildings which were not the Lieutenant's responsibility are conspicuously absent from the plan.

[71] There is no reason to suppose the 'plotte' as originally commissioned would not have included the Liberty, which Peyton clearly felt to be part of his domain as Lieutenant of the Tower.

[72] For an extremely useful précis of Haiward's work, see P. Eden *et al.*, *A Dictionary of Land Surveyors,* second edition (London, 1998), H250; for his Fenland career see R. J. Silvester, 'William Haiwarde and the Fens', *Fenland Research*, 6 (1989), pp. 38-42. I am grateful to Dr Sarah Bendall for sharing with me her unpublished information on William Haiward.

[73] For another of Haiward's more far-flung projects, see H. Taylor, 'A Report on the 1614 Survey of the Lordship of Hartington, Derbyshire', unpublished report for the Peak District National Park Archaeological Service, 1998.

[74] Although Peyton was born in Kent, by the mid-1580s he was well established in Norfolk, and was described as 'of Outwell', near Wisbech. Hassell Smith and Baker (eds.), *The Papers of Nathaniel Bacon of Stiffkey*, II and III.

[75] Holkham Hall, Davidson Catalogue, Longham 472, 14 October 1583.

[76] E. Lynam, 'Early maps of the Fen district', *The Geographical Journal* 84:5 (November 1934), pp. 420-3; T. Badeslade, *The History of the Ancient and Present State of the Navigation of the Ports of King's-Lyn and of Cambridge* (London, 1725), pp. 10, 23, 119; W. Dugdale, *The History of Imbanking and Drayning of Divers Fenns and Marshes* (London, 1662), p. 382.

[77] The 'Orders for the Governmt of the Tower' of 1555 refer to 'sourveyors' as among the castle's personnel, PRO SP11/6, f. 50. The remarkable series of surveys produced by Saxton in the years 1574-9 also appear to have been a government initiative.

[78] Holkham Hall 92/5, remarkably the draught of this plan also survives: Holkham 91/5. See also Haiward's 1591 map of Marshland, published in *East Anglia Archaeology* 45 (1988), p. 10, which is strikingly similar in appearance to the Longham map. The Longham survey is undated, and it is just possible that Peyton was involved in its creation: he both owned land there and was involved in a dispute over the boundaries of the parish of Longham in 1593. In 1595 he sold lands at Longham and Tittleshall to Sir Edward Coke; plans of both these places by William Haiward survive at Holkham Hall. Holkham Hall, Davidson Catalogue, Longham 533, 551.

[79] Though they share an unusual surname, there is nothing more which obviously connects him to the surveyor and cartographer Joel Gascoyne (1650-1705) who was born in Hull and whose father, one Thomas Gascoyne, was a master mariner; C. S. Nicholls, *The Dictionary of National Biography: Missing Persons* (Oxford and New York, 1993), p. 245.

[80] Perhaps he was the John Gascoigne of St Botolph's outside Aldersgate, who died in November 1626, and whose wife, Jane, was then granted the administration of his estate valued at £20, PRO, PROB 6/12, f. 109r.

[81] 'Register of St Peter ad Vincula, Tower of London', ff. 88r-90v, 117r, 119v. Raiph Gascoyne was certainly involved in the boundary dispute with the City, and was called upon to prove some of the Tower's claims, PRO, WO55/1776, f. 57r.

[82] John Norden, in his *Surveiors Dialogue* (London, 1618), p. 23, emphasized the importance to a surveyor of having assistance from those long resident in the area being surveyed.

# III. THE ACCURACY OF THE PLAN

## Introduction

To try to establish whether this hypothesis for the origin of the plan is correct and to assess its reliability as a historical source, it is essential that the accuracy of the survey be established. While one might hesitate to read too much into apparently incidental details on a plan made solely to settle a boundary dispute, if the plan was conceived to illustrate a statement on the purpose of the fortress and its governor, and only subsequently used as evidence in a jurisdictional dispute, then those details cease to be incidental and become much more interesting.

The format of the survey is essentially that of a *plan cavalier*, that is to say a ground plan which has been turned into a drawing showing external details by using the plan as the base from which to draw up vertical lines to form the exterior of buildings. The ground plan is drawn from a measured survey, whereas the elevational detail seems to have been done more or less freehand. Again, of course, it is important to stress that, unfortunately, we cannot work from the original; the closest we can currently get to it is the Robert Whitehand copy of January 1712/13 which, for the time being, can only be assumed to be an accurate copy of the original survey.

The accuracy of the Haiward and Gascoyne plan was considered by laying over it a modern survey of the site to the same scale, and aligning them in a way which allowed the greatest agreement between the two.

## The Liberty and the City

It seems probable that were William Haiward and John Gascoyne to find themselves within the Tower of London today, they would recognize their surroundings, but they would be hard-pressed to recognize the areas outside the Tower such as Nine Gardens or East Smithfield. Establishing the accuracy of their record of the environs of the Tower, and in particular the line of the Liberty is, therefore, very difficult, as not only have many of the buildings which defined the Liberty disappeared, but the plan itself is our only visual source for the position of that line in the period before the Commonwealth.

Several landmarks do survive, though, and these give some indication of the topographical precision of the plan in its depiction of the environs of the Tower. The remains of the Roman city wall are shown in exactly the same position as is recorded on the modern Ordnance Survey, this is also the case with the street called the 'Way from Aldgate', now known as Minories. The Haiward and Gascoyne plan is less accurate on the western side where All Hallows, Barking ('Barkin Church'), though it is shown sitting partly on its actual site, is a little too far south, as is also the case with 'Tower Street'. However, this does not distort the general outline of the plan on this side, and the river front is correctly located. The accuracy of the eastern side of the Liberty is extremely difficult to confirm as the historic topography has been destroyed by Tower Bridge approach road. It was here that the line of the Liberty in 1597 must have followed most closely the edge of the moat, which was revetted with a brick wall in the early 1680s. Unfortunately, no substantial landmarks survive in this area today which can be compared to the Haiward and Gascoyne survey.

It is clear that no real attempt was made to represent accurately on the 1597 plan the appearance of most of the buildings and landscape either of Tower Hill and around the moat or of the City and St Katharine's. The Haiward and Gascoyne plan gives the impression that the environs of the Tower were, on the whole, rural expanses broken only occasionally by a line or huddle of houses. In reality, of course, this was far from the truth. Numerous contemporary sources show much of the area surrounding the Liberty of the Tower to have been a positive jungle of buildings of all shapes and sizes (Fig. 7).[83] The features which are represented are there to locate and define the boundary; thus Petty Wales, Tower Street, Pike's Garden, London Wall, the Postern, Hog Lane and St Katharine's are shown and named, as are notable landmarks such as the scaffold and the cross. Much the same can be said of the landscape shown within the Liberty: a contemporary plan at Hatfield House indicates that the area called 'Nine Gardens' was more built-up than this survey suggests.[84] The lack of detail shown on the buildings by the City Ditch make it quite clear that the plan's purpose was not to rail against the erection of buildings in that area, which was a common cause for vociferous complaint in these decades.

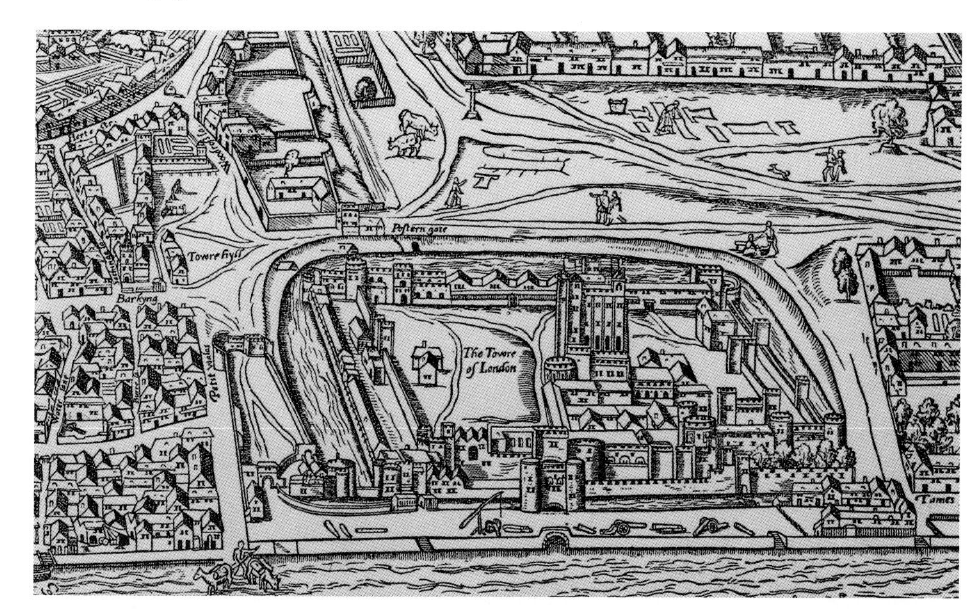


Fig. 7. Detail of the mid-sixteenth-century 'Agas' map of London.
(The Guildhall Library, Corporation of London)

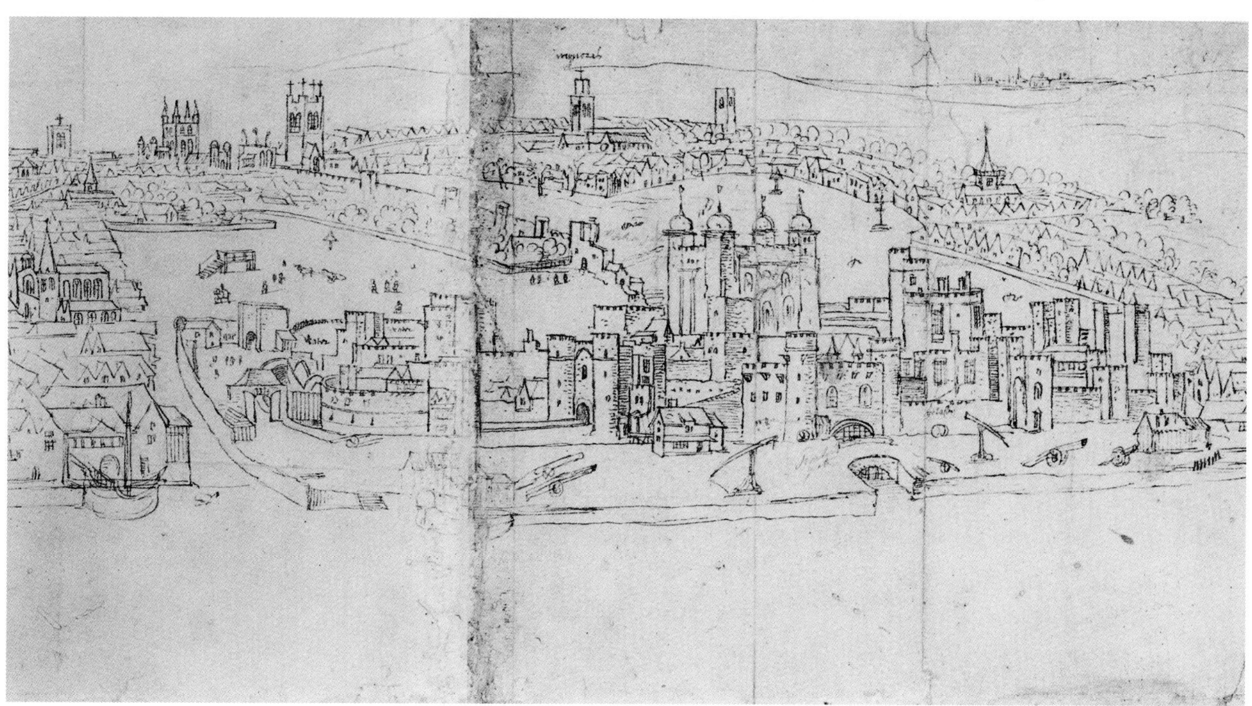

Fig. 8. View of the Tower of London from the panorama of London by Anthonis van den Wyngaerde of *c.* 1544.
(Ashmolean Museum, Oxford)

## The curtain walls and the wharf

The line of the outer and inner curtain walls and the wharf featured on the plan is, on the whole, remarkably accurate. This is relatively straightforward to judge as these structures have remained largely unchanged in outline since the Middle Ages. For the outer curtain wall on the north, east and west sides of the Tower, the line of the battlement was apparently intended to represent the ground-line of the wall. In the case of the inner curtain wall and the southern range of the outer curtain the ground line of the wall is more precisely shown by the base of the wall drawn on the plan rather than the line of the crenellations on top. The position of these walls is, in general, accurately shown: the distance between what is now called Legge's Mount and the Develin Tower, spanning the whole diagonal width of the Tower, is accurately represented on the survey. This is also true of the distance across the centre of the Tower from Broad Arrow to Beauchamp and from Bowyer to Wakefield.

Fig. 9. The Tower of London from the Thames in about 1660 by Wenceslaus Hollar.
(© Copyright The British Museum (1859-8-6-389))

Fig. 10. The Tower of London from a late fifteenth-century book of poems by Charles, Duke of Orléans.
(By permission of the British Library (Roy 16 F II f. 73))

There are areas of notable inaccuracy, however: the Martin Tower and the Brass Mount are shown too far south-west on the survey but the extent of distortion is limited and has not corrupted the rest of the plan. The southern outer curtain wall between the Byward and Well towers is shown some six metres too far north, and the Lion Tower is depicted smaller and further north than was actually the case. There are, therefore, areas of significant inaccuracy, but these are isolated and on the whole the positioning of the outer and inner curtain walls and the wharf is remarkable in its precision. The internal angles of the walls are almost always right to within 2° or 3° and none of the areas of significant inaccuracy is allowed to distort the overall footprint of the Tower.

As has been discussed above, it seems that the plan-makers were little interested in giving realistic representations of buildings outside the Tower. This is less true of the way the wharf is shown; not only does the shape and position accord very closely with what is there today, but here there is greater detail of the appearance of the structure and its contents. The survey depicts the landing stairs, cranes, cannon and houses on the eastern end, all of which are known from other sources to have been there (Figs. 7 and 8).[85] A comparison of the house by the Byward postern as shown in the 1597 plan (Col. Pl. 2) with Wyngaerde's depiction of that feature on his panorama of around 1544 (Fig. 8), demonstrates that although the former is schematic it does share the basic form of the Wyngaerde house.[86]

## Internal features of the Tower

It has been remarked above that the positioning of the curtain walls and towers is on the whole remarkably accurate on the Haiward and Gascoyne plan. This is also true of the internal features. Many of these do not survive, but from those that do we can see something of the strengths and weaknesses of the survey in this respect. The Chapel of St Peter ad Vincula is shown as exactly the right length but is located some six metres or so too far east, and while the White Tower also rises up from a footprint of the right size and shape, it too is placed five metres or so too far to the east. The position of the wall running between the Wakefield Tower and the Coldharbour Gate is, however, very precisely plotted, as is the 'Queens' gallery.

One of the great attractions of the Haiward and Gascoyne plan is that it shows a wealth of detail of the buildings within the Tower, of which so little is known from other sources. However, it is crucial to establish to what extent these details are accurate and faithfully recorded, and to what extent schematic or even fantastic. Again, it is very difficult to tell in most cases as the building does not survive, or at any rate has been dramatically altered since the sixteenth century. However, a few specific comparisons should serve to give some indication.

The area of the medieval royal lodgings facing the river from St Thomas's Tower to the Lanthorn Tower is shown in several early images and partly survives today. The mid-seventeenth-century drawing by Wenceslaus Hollar (Fig. 9) and the illumination from the Orléans manuscript in the British Library (Fig. 10) both show the square lodging block to the east of the Wakefield Tower. These two sources agree on the general appearance of this building of which two storeys are visible: it has a crenellated roof, the upper floor contains two elaborate windows, each with four lights, the lower floor also contains some more quite substantial windows, although it is difficult to say how many as the outer curtain wall obscures the view. In comparison, the Haiward and Gascoyne plan, while it does show a square lodging block with crenellated roof in this position and indicates the presence of the windows, the scale and detail of these is not communicated, only a slight indication that those on the upper storey were composed of more than one light. It is perhaps worth noting, as well, that when making his engraving of the plan, the engraver left out these windows altogether.[87] The same simplistic way of recording the details of buildings is displayed in the area of the Wakefield Tower as in the sketch of the house on the wharf mentioned above.

Another area and another source also bear out this judgement on Haiward and Gascoyne's pictorial representation of buildings within the Tower. The row of houses on the west of the wall running north from the Wakefield Tower to the Coldharbour Gate is shown in a drawing by T. H. Shepherd made in the mid-nineteenth century (Fig. 11). If this drawing is compared to the 1597 plan (Col. Pl. 2), it is clear that what the latter shows is a very rudimentary representation of the row of buildings, the seven gables looking more like seven separate houses than one continuous row.

That the plan combines rather schematic images with very accurate ones is demonstrated by a comparison between the Lieutenant's lodgings as shown by Haiward and Gascoyne (Col. Pl. 2) and by Wenceslaus Hollar on his mid-seventeenth-century drawing of the Tower (Fig. 9). Hollar shows the line of battlements between the Lieutenant's lodgings and the Bloody Tower, the gable ends of the lodging rising out of the curtain wall and the windows: a small and a large window in the eastern gable and a prominent gothic window in the central gable. In all these details, the Haiward and Gascoyne plan accords with the Hollar drawing.

Therefore, it seems that although the Haiward and Gascoyne survey does not always accurately depict some of the features of the buildings it shows, it does give a very sound picture of their overall form and position, and sometimes of their architectural details. That it is not always reliable is indicated by the physical impossibility of the positioning of the west end of the hall and of the buildings in other areas, such as the houses on the west side of the inner curtain wall adjacent to the label for 'The Mint', and the obvious omissions and inaccuracies such as the windows and roof of the White Tower. However, something of the extraordinary importance of this plan is indicated by the fact that even very minor buildings like the house

Fig. 11. The row of houses running north from the Wakefield Tower drawn by T. H. Shepherd just before their demolition in 1846.

(The Guildhall Library, Corporation of London)

on the wharf by the Byward postern were apparently drawn from life. It should also be remembered that Haiward and Gascoyne's work is here being measured against modern standards of mapping, and that it was made when accurate drawn surveys were extremely rare. Not only was it to be eighty-five years until a new measured survey of the fortress — the 'Plan of the Tower and Liberties' of 1682 — was taken, but even this was unable to improve on the measured accuracy of its sixteenth-century forebear.[88]

It is also worth remarking on the written detail given on the plan. It is noticeable that, with the exception of the Mint, the buildings in the Tower which were not within the Lieutenant's jurisdiction were not labelled.[89] The great sweep of buildings belonging to the Ordnance Office, though represented, is completely unidentified on the plan. The structures which are named are the defensive towers of the fortress, the buildings and garden of the royal palace and the Lieutenant's own lodgings. This would make complete sense if the survey were drawn up to accompany Peyton's report on his responsibilities as Lieutenant of the Tower, as there would — in that case — have been no particular purpose in naming buildings for which he was not answerable.

The degrees of accuracy in the 1597 plan, therefore, seem to vary in a way which is consistent with the suggestion that the plan was both an illustration of the Lieutenant's charges and a document submitted to a committee considering the status of the Liberty. A consistent level of detail in the depiction of the position or fenestration of the buildings for which the Lieutenant was responsible would not have been of vital importance, though an impression of their scale and function might well have been.

## NOTES

[83] 'The Procession of Edward VI ... engraved from a painting at Cowdray' at the Society of Antiquaries; the 'Agas' map of *c.* 1560-70 (Fig. 7); the Wyngaerde 'Panorama' of *c.* 1544 (Fig. 8); and the William Smith panorama of 1588, to mention a few.

[84] G. Parnell, 'Five seventeenth-century plans of the Tower of London' *London Topographical Record* XXV (1980), pp. 66-9. On this point, it is interesting to note that the Hatfield House plan, of similar date to the Haiward and Gascoyne survey, seems to bear no relation to that survey. This might be a reason for considering whether in fact the Hatfield plan precedes the Haiward and Gascoyne in date. Debates over the building encroachments by the City Ditch which probably generated the Hatfield plan were taking place in the 1590s as well as in 1606, see, e.g., *APC*, XX, p. 58.

[85] The cannon and cranes can be seen on the wharf in several sources, as can the cluster of houses at the east end; see also the entry for the wharf in the Gazetteer at the end of this volume.

[86] H. Colvin and S. Foister (eds.), *The Panorama of London circa 1544 by Anthonis van den Wyngaerde* London Topographical Society publication 151 (London, 1996), p. 37. Both show a house of two blocks, a main building with a smaller annexe on the east gable end. But whereas Wyngaerde shows the dormer window on the first floor, the door and window on the ground floor, two gable windows and a window on the annexe, it is clear that Haiward and Gascoyne's representation is only a simplified version of this — the shape of the building is the same but little attempt is made to show the windows realistically.

[87] This same trend can be seen again in the case of the annexe on the southern wall of the White Tower. Here both Hollar and the Orléans manuscript show a square block, with a crenellated top, which has on its south face a large double-light window. The 1597 plan also shows a squarish block in this position, and a two-light window is just visible towards the top of the building — but this is recorded with little of the detail or clarity of the other two images.

[88] Parnell, 'Five seventeenth-century plans of the Tower of London', pp. 72-9.

[89] In this respect it might seem surprising that the Haiward and Gascoyne plan (always assuming it was as the Whitehand copy represents it) does include a label for the Mint. However, though it was not strictly his domain, Peyton was greatly interested in the Mint: at the end of the third version of his 'declaracon' he added a paper on improving its operation, for which he gave the justification that: 'although in office distinct from my chardge', the Mint was 'w$^{th}$ in y$^{e}$ Jurisdiction of this command', Bod. Lib., MS Eng Hist e 195, f. 7r. The Whitehand and Heath copies show a dotted line running right round the Outer Ward perhaps included to mark the limits of the Mint's jurisdiction.

# IV. THE PLAN IN THE SEVENTEENTH AND EIGHTEENTH CENTURIES

EVIDENCE for the fate of the Haiward and Gascoyne plan in the seventeenth century rests partly in its influence on subsequent plans of the Tower. Following the Great Fire of London several schemes were drawn up for significantly improving the Tower's fortifications; some of the plans which illustrate these were almost certainly copied from the 1597 survey. Endorsed by Sir Bernard de Gomme, Chief Engineer of the Ordnance, a plan of 1666 which proposed an ambitious new addition to the western entrance of the Tower, is obviously closely related to the Haiward and Gascoyne survey.[90] The perspective of the de Gomme plan is the same as Haiward and Gascoyne's, the mural towers which de Gomme illustrates are of the same form as those on the 1597 plan, and the detailing of the whole of the western entrance, in particular the Byward Tower, is lifted straight from Haiward and Gascoyne's work. Indeed, the de Gomme outline of the Tower and wharf, with a few inconsistencies, seems to have been traced directly from the 1597 survey.[91] That this is likely to have been the case is confirmed by another very similar plan, drawn up in around 1667, which also illustrated proposed alterations to the defences of the Tower (Fig. 12). This time the connection to the 1597 survey is explicit: in the top left corner of the plan are the words 'A Coppy of m^r^ Hewards Mapp verifyed by Jonas Moore'.[92] This firmly establishes both that the Haiward and Gascoyne survey was still accessible to the Ordnance Office in 1667 and, therefore, probably at the Tower of London, and that it remained the best plan of the Tower available to the Ordnance draughtsmen.

Two other late seventeenth-century plans also owe something to Haiward and Gascoyne. The first is the map of London after the fire of 1666 engraved by Wenceslaus Hollar. The representation of the Tower on this is by no means a straight copy of the 1597 survey, as is shown by its rendering of the western entrance; however, the perspective of the view and the form of the roof of the White Tower — among other things — are strongly reminiscent of the earlier survey. If Hollar did not actually trace from the Haiward and Gascoyne survey, as Jonas Moore had done, he very likely used it as a guide. The other plan which seems to relate to Haiward and Gascoyne's work is the Holcroft Blood view of 1688 (Fig. 13), which is similar in aspect to the Haiward and Gascoyne survey and which seems to have been as visually elaborate as the 1597 plan must have been, described as featuring 'Guilding & ornam:^ts^' which took '4 Moneths time' to complete.[93] However, the resemblance is superficial, being one of general viewpoint rather than of detail or proportions.

In addition to the evidence of the influence of the Haiward and Gascoyne survey on later plans of the Tower, there are also signs that it was still being referred to in quarrels about the Liberty in the reign of Charles II. The boundary disputes had rumbled on through the seventeenth century and when, in 1678, the court leet of the Tower gave a variety of rulings on what was and was not within the Liberty, it ruled 'according to the old Draught drawn Eighty yeares agoe As by the Mapp appears'.[94] This reference to a map of the Tower Liberties of *c.* 1598 indicates that in the 1670s the Haiward and Gascoyne survey was still being used as a current statement of the extent of the Tower's authority. It may be that the 'Mapp of the Tower and Liberty', cited as evidence that Tower Hill was within the Tower Liberty in 1683, was also the 1597 survey.[95]

The reign of James II saw the re-definition both of the privileges allowed to inhabitants of the Liberty of the Tower and of the extent of the Liberty itself — which was now formally enlarged to include the Minories, the Old Artillery Ground and Well Close. With this it seems probable that the Haiward and Gascoyne plan was, for practical purposes at least, considered of little use.[96]

Robert Whitehand's copy of the survey was dated January 1712(/13), but, as has been mentioned above, his reason for copying the sixteenth-century survey then is unclear. It does indicate that the plan was still at the Tower of London at this time. Although the survey had been commissioned by the Lieutenant and not the Master-General of the Ordnance, it seems likely that with the establishment of a drawing office in the fortress, provided with ample accommodation in the eastern annexe of the White Tower, the original drawing would have been housed here. After this, it is not until

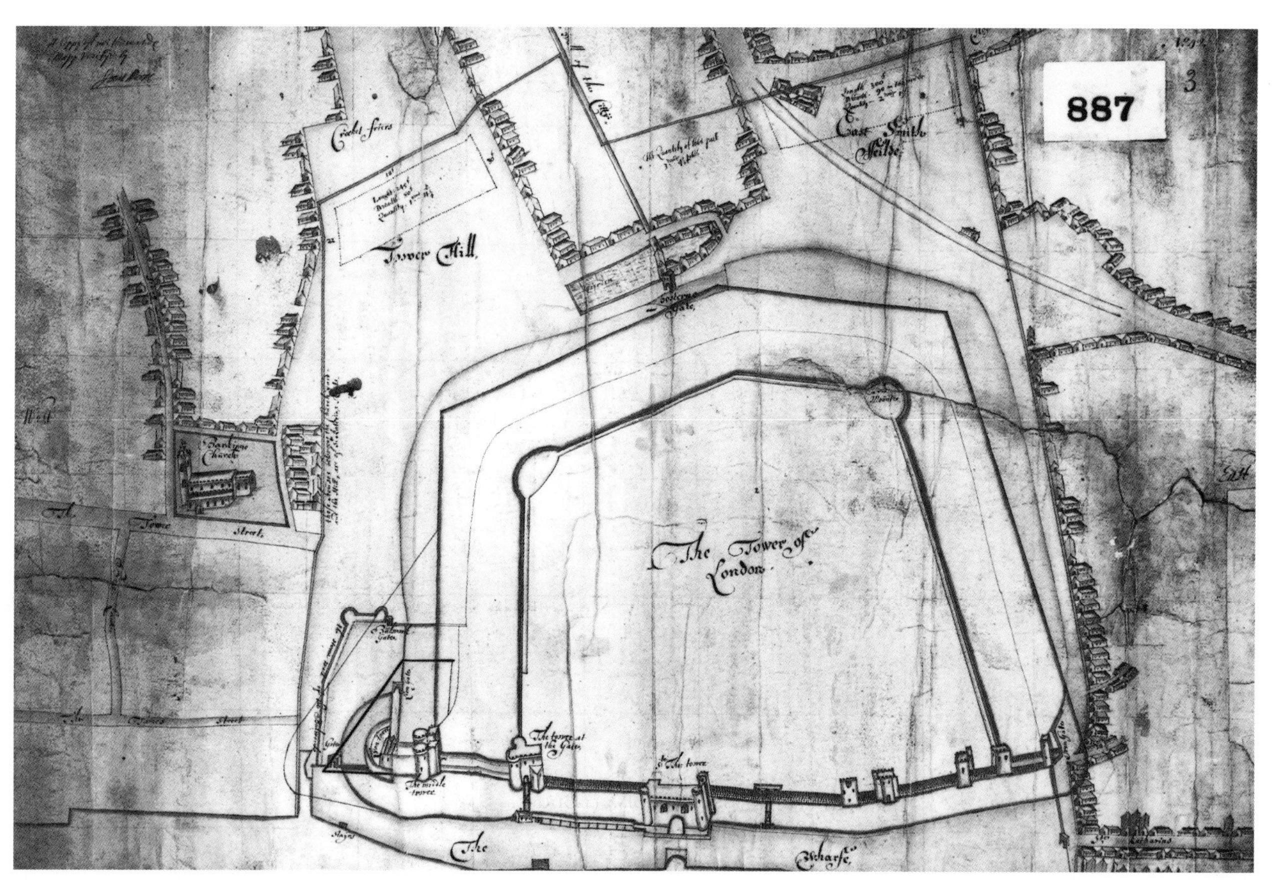


Fig. 12. A plan of the Tower and Liberty endorsed by Sir Jonas Moore, *c.* 1667. (The Public Record Office (WORK 31/21))

May 1741, when Clement Lemprière made his copy and George Vertue brought the plan to the Society of Antiquaries, that we hear of it again.

John, second Duke of Montagu (1688?-1749), was a soldier and a courtier in the reigns of the first two Hanoverian kings.[97] In the course of his life he twice held the post of Master-General of the Ordnance: from 1740 to 1742 and again from 1742 to 1749, and it was presumably in this capacity that he came across the Haiward and Gascoyne survey.[98] As well as being active in public affairs, Montagu was patron and friend of the distinguished antiquarian William Stukeley. Although Stukeley was given to eulogy on the subject of his sponsor, his praise of the Duke is still telling: 'we had exactly the same taste for old family concerns, genealogys, pictures, furniture, coats of arms, the old way of building, gardening & the like; in a general imitation of pure nature, in the gothic architecture ...'.[99] Montagu, whose particular interest was military architecture, seems to have enjoyed the company of Stukeley and together the two men visited historic sites and frequently exchanged antiquities.[100] Stukeley noted in his diary that although Montagu 'was no scholar himself', he 'has a proper sense of the value of these antiquitys'.[101]

Although there is no concrete evidence of the sequence of events, it is possible to speculate that in his capacity as Master-General of the Ordnance, the Duke of Montagu saw the Haiward and Gascoyne plan, perhaps even in the Drawing Room, and realised, with his 'proper sense of the value of these antiquitys', that what was of little interest as a working survey of the Tower was of great interest as a historic record of the ancient royal castle and palace.[102] Having stumbled upon such a treasure he might have commissioned Clement Lemprière to make a copy and, once this was finished or well under way, lent the original to George Vertue, to whom he knew it would be of interest.[103] If this was indeed what happened, the Duke would have had to have found the plan within the first year of his tenure as Master-General; this would, in some ways, make sense as it would explain why he decided to bring the plan to the notice of the Antiquaries in spring 1741 and why two copies were made in such

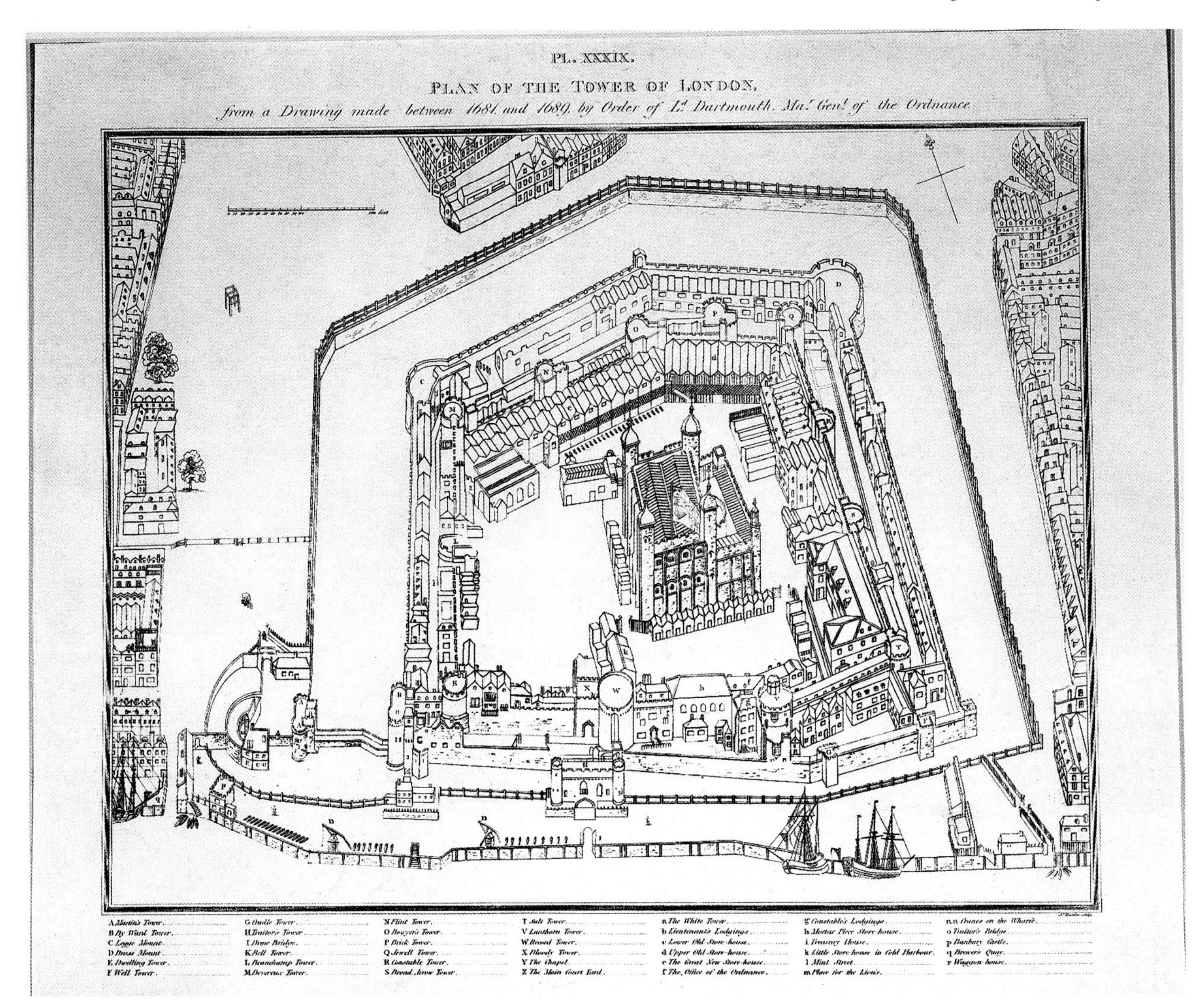


Fig. 13. Bird's-eye-view of the Tower in 1688 by Holcroft Blood, as engraved in 1815. (© Historic Royal Palaces)

quick succession. Sadly, though, after 1741, when the Antiquaries took their copy, the trail runs cold. A list of the plans belonging to the Ordnance Drawing Room taken in 1743 refers only to Whitehand's copy of the survey, and not to the original version, suggesting that the 1597 original did not return there.[104] It is not known, though, what did happen to it: whether the Duke took the plan into his care as Master-General elsewhere in the Tower, whether it passed into the Duke's personal collection at Boughton or Montagu House, or indeed whether it went somewhere else altogether. It seems unlikely that, having so impressed the Antiquaries with his plan, the Duke of Montagu would then have discarded it; however, the plan does not appear to have passed into the collection of the Duke of Buccleuch with much of the rest of Montagu's collection, and its whereabouts are now unknown.[105]

## NOTES

[90] Parnell, 'Five seventeenth-century plans of the Tower of London', pp. 69-70.

[91] I am grateful to Jeremy Ashbee for pointing this out.

[92] PRO, WORK 31/21; Parnell, 'Five-seventeenth century plans of the Tower of London', pp. 70-2.

[93] PRO, WO51/36, f. 144r. I am grateful to Geoffrey Parnell for pointing out the similarities between the two plans.

[94] CLRO, Misc. MSS 171/1, 'The Answer of the Court Leet of the Tower to the Complaintes of the Inquest of

Tower Street Ward &c. 10th October 1678'. This document also refers to 'Dr Goads Buildings Survey' being consulted; it is unclear what this was: whether it was a drawn rather that a written survey and whether it was made in the later sixteenth rather than the seventeenth century. References to a Dr Roger Goad can be found in the City papers for Elizabeth I's reign, but this Dr Goad was provost of King's College, Cambridge, and there is nothing which immediately suggests that he had anything to do with the boundary disputes between the City and the Tower. A copy of the document is to be found in CLRO, Misc. MSS 33/15; I am grateful to Stephen Priestley for pointing it out to me. See also PRO, WO55/1776, f. 41r for the Tower court leet referring to 'severall very old surveys & Mapps' of the Liberty.

[95] CLRO, Misc. MSS 171/1, 'The Case of Inhabitants within his Majesties Royalty of the Tower of London ... 17 May 1683'. It is possible, though, that the map referred to was the survey of the Tower executed the previous year.

[96] See Lipman, 'The jurisdiction of the Tower authorities', in Charlton (ed.), *The Tower of London*, pp. 147-9.

[97] I am extremely grateful to Rachel Watson of the Northampton Record Office for her kind assistance and advice on the second Duke of Montagu, and for trawling the Record Office for any trace of Haiward and Gascoyne's original plan.

[98] O. F. G. Hogg, *The Royal Arsenal*, 2 vols. (London, 1963), I, pp. 347, 350; II, p. 1037.

[99] W. C. Lukis (ed.), *The Family Memoirs of the Rev. William Stukeley*, 3 vols. (Durham, 1882-7), I, p. 114.

[100] See, for example, ibid., I, pp. 89, 367, 382.

[101] Ibid., I, p. 77; III, p. 172.

[102] That the Duke considered the Tower, and his position there as Master-General of the Ordnance, important is illustrated by the 1749 portrait of him by Thomas Hudson, in which the White Tower stands prominently in the background. The fact that the Duke himself was credited as designer/surveyor of a plan of proposed barracks at Woolwich of 1741, indicates that he knew something of surveying and draughtsmanship, PRO, WO55/2281, f. 36r.

[103] This does slightly raise the question of why Lemprière needed to make a new copy when the Whitehand copy was presumably still in the Drawing Room. It may be, as he had requested in his will, that Whitehand's plan was used in the instruction of young draughtsmen, and that Lemprière's copy was taken to replace the 'master' or original once it had been removed. Joseph Heath's copy of the survey of 1752 may have been made as an exercise in draughtsmanship.

[104] PRO, WO55/2281, ff. 28v-29r.

[105] I am extremely grateful to the following people for their assistance in the (as yet unsuccessful) hunt for the original survey: the Duke of Buccleuch; A. Fisher, archivist at Drumlanrig Castle; Rachel Watson of the Northampton Record Office; Mrs Edward Brudenell of Deene Park; Susan Tomkins, archivist at Beaulieu; the staff of the National Register of Archives.

## V. CONCLUSIONS: THE VALUE OF THE SURVEY

As has been discussed above, although the Haiward and Gascoyne plan has shortcomings as a source for the history of the Tower of London, the schematic nature of its representation of some aspects of the castle should not obscure its general accuracy, which is particularly remarkable given its early date. The plan is an extraordinary source for any study of the history of the Tower before the castle was transformed by the Ordnance Office in the late seventeenth century. The magnitude of the changes which were to take place in the century following this commission has been well attested to.[106] As a result, the Haiward and Gascoyne survey is our only visual source for an area which in 1597 was still (in theory at least) a functioning royal palace, with hall, jewel house, privy gallery, wardrobe and royal lodgings. By the time the next plan of any comparable detail was made, these buildings had all been demolished or transformed beyond recognition — indeed a deliberate policy of clearing the Inner Ward had been undertaken by the Ordnance Office in an attempt to modernise the Tower for military use.

The plan gives a final glimpse of the Tower before the destruction of the royal palace which, though it was already in a pretty desperate state, was suffering from neglect rather than the wilful dismantling that was to be its fate in the seventeenth century. It is invaluable for the geography of the fortress and, in particular, for locating specific buildings within the Inner Ward; without it we would be struggling for any certainty about the position of the Tudor jewel houses, the lodgings where the principal royal rooms were to be found or the hall. If the Haiward and Gascoyne plan had not survived, it would be possible to hypothesise about these buildings, but the beauty of the plan is that as well as depicting them it positively identifies them by name and function. As a combination of drawn survey with bird's-eye-view, Haiward and Gascoyne's work is extraordinarily important: it reveals not only the position and plan of buildings, but their appearance and form as well. Having said this, it should be borne in mind that though the pictorial detail of the plan is often revealing and accurate, it is in places simplistic and the survey should be treated carefully in this respect.

More than this, the lack of clarity enveloping the status of the area surrounding the Tower from which the 1597 plan was born has endured. In the autumn of 1997 the Treasury Solicitor was asked to consider the question 'Who owns Tower Hill?', and the answer seems to be no less complicated than it was in the 1590s. If the hypothesis posited above is accepted, that the Haiward and Gascoyne plan was submitted to a committee considering the Liberty issue, then it should also be seen as the earliest of many such plans which illustrate the legal or quasi-legal boundaries of the locality, and as one of the earlier documents of any description to contribute to the matter.[107] The lack of complete certainty on the issue today makes this, the oldest extant plan to try to establish the boundary conclusively, even more valuable. It means that the survey has never been rendered completely obsolete in its function as evidence intended to aid the resolution of a jurisdictional ambiguity; that ambiguity perseveres and no full consideration of it is complete without reference to Haiward and Gascoyne's work of some four hundred years ago.

### NOTES

[106] G. Parnell, 'The Tower of London: the reconstruction of the Inmost Ward during the reign of Charles II', *Transactions of the London and Middlesex Archaeological Society* (1980) XXXI, pp. 147–56'.

[107] Its successors include the 1682 'Dartmouth survey', the post-1686 map of the Tower Liberties which includes the three areas outside the old Liberty, reproduced in Charlton (ed.), *The Tower of London*, p. 148; and the later PRO, WO94/72/17.

# VI. A GAZETTEER OF THE PRINCIPAL BUILDINGS OF THE TOWER OF LONDON SHOWN ON THE HAIWARD AND GASCOYNE SURVEY

THE purpose of the following gazetteer is to summarise what is known from documentary sources of the buildings of the Tower of London and their function when it was mapped by William Haiward and John Gascoyne. Its focus is, therefore, the history of the buildings in the century before the survey was made. It does not cover the buildings of the Liberty or beyond shown on the survey, and — with one or two exceptions — it does not concern itself with buildings not labelled on the 1597 survey. It makes no attempt to add to the excellent work which has been done by others on the medieval Tower. Unless otherwise indicated, references to the Haiward and Gascoyne survey are to the Robert Whitehand copy of January 1712/13 (Col. Pl. 2), which, as is explained above, is the most accurate copy of the missing original.

The name and letter which refer to a building on the Whitehand version of the 1597 survey are given in bold italics. Where it differs from the sixteenth-century nomenclature, the modern name for a building is given in upper case bold.

### *The Bulwark gate*

In his late sixteenth-century *Survey of London* John Stow recorded that 'Edward IV. fortified the Tower of London, and enclosed within brick, as is aforesaid, a certain piece of ground taken out of the Tower Hill, west from the Lion Tower, now called the bulwark'.[1] That the enclosure was his work is confirmed by the payment made in around 1480 of £16 for making 'the bulwark' at the Tower.[2] Almost immediately the enclosure had its own caretaker: on 9 March 1484 one Thomas Redehede was appointed 'keeper of the "Bulwerk" without the western gate of the Tower of London for term of his life'.[3] At the time of its construction the Bulwark was visually remarkable by being built from brick, a fact frequently mentioned in references to it, one chronicler even calling it 'the Redd Bulwark'.[4]

Given the disputed nature of the Tower Liberties, the gate which gave access to the Bulwark from Tower Hill was in this period the *de facto* entrance to the Tower and the place where its certain jurisdiction began: it was here that the young Edward VI was received by the Lieutenant and Constable of the Tower on 31 January 1547, and here that the sheriffs of London received prisoners when they were taken from the Tower for execution.[5] The security of the Bulwark was of the highest importance: guns were placed about the walls,[6] while access to it was via two great gateways: that to the north (to which the label 'The Bulwark gate' on the 1597 survey properly applies) and that to the south which led on to the wharf.[7]

As the 'gate of the first entry' to the Tower, the Bulwark also saw the passage of countless people in and out of the fortress, and shops which provided for them operated within the enclosure. In Mary I's reign this was considered an insufferable risk to the security of the castle and orders were issued for the daytime ward house to be moved to the Bulwark, and for the shops there to be closed. These orders were not implemented and in Elizabeth I's reign were reduced simply to a stipulation that foreign shopkeepers should not stay overnight in the Bulwark.[8]

While the Wyngaerde drawing of *c.* 1544 shows the Bulwark bounded simply by a wall on the western side (Fig. 8), the 1597 plan shows a great snake of buildings to have grown up along its line, indicating that there was a significant expansion in the number of houses within the enclosure during the century. This was a cause of great concern to Sir John Peyton, who complained of the increase in such buildings which 'have byn in former tymes ... demised unto the warders, officers and artificers belonginge unto the Tower, But of late inhabited by Strangers manie of them being very poore & disordred persons'.[9] Nothing above ground now remains of the Bulwark enclosure, which was demolished between 1668 and 1680.[10]

### *The Lyons Tower* and *y*[e] *Lyons gate*

The large semicircular barbican, which came to be home to the Tower menagerie, was built in 1276–8 as part of Edward I's additions to the Tower of London's fortifications; the enclosed space within it was being used to house the royal collection of exotic animals from the 1330s at least. The gateway to the north of the barbican, or Lion Tower, reached by a bridge across the moat was apparently built at the same time and is styled 'y[e] Lyons gate' on the 1597 survey.[11]

The Lion Tower remained essentially unaltered in form during the sixteenth century. The estimate for works probably made in 1532 provided only for 'The Lyon towre to be Roughcast w$^{t}$ lyme', though among the appended list of necessary repairs which had not yet been started was: 'The lyons Towre to haue newe Roofes and new florys'; however, there is no sign that either of these were included in the works campaign which followed.[12] What did receive attention in the 1530s building works, however, was the 'Brydge by the lyon Towere', running north to the 'Lyons Gate', which had itself been rebuilt thirty years earlier.[13] The bridge was provided with 70 foot of 'crestes and coynes', while masons were employed 'Turnyng of An arche for the enlarging of the corn$^{r}$ of the Brydge', and 124 yards of paving was installed between the Tower and the gate.[14] This smartening-up of the entrance to the Tower was among those works carried out in haste in the month preceding the coronation of Anne Boleyn on 1 June 1533, and was no doubt done to ensure an impressive starting point for the new Queen's great procession from the Tower through the City to Whitehall. That the works were largely cosmetic is also suggested by the fact that a report on the ordnance at the Tower made less than three years later considered that the 'two bridges at the Lyon gate ... require repair'.[15] The bridges do not seem to have received the proper attention they needed until well into Elizabeth's reign, when the accounts for 1581–2 record payments 'for makinge two new bridges for Cairr by the Lyonns house and the Towre gate'.[16]

The Keeper of the Lions had a lodging within the Tower and it seems likely that this was the gabled house shown in the south-east corner of the enclosure on Haiward and Gascoyne's survey.[17] This was a building of at least two storeys with a tiled roof, which was provided with new floors in 1583/4, and was re-tiled and had its four chimneys reconstructed in 1602–3.[18]

The animals kept in the Lion Tower were a hugely popular tourist attraction. In 1515 the Venetian diplomat Peter Pasqualigio was shown lions and leopards; in 1544 the Duke of Nagera saw four lions and two leopards in wooden cages; while when Thomas Platter visited in 1599, he noted a porcupine and tigers, as well as the lions, one of which nearly injured Platter's servant when it pushed its claws through the bars of the cage.[19] The menagerie was not just open to visiting dignitaries: two distinguished visitors to the imprisoned Catholic priest John Gerard gained entry to the Tower by dressing as 'simple London citizens' and pretending they wanted to 'visit the lions that are kept in the Tower and the other animals which curious people come to see'.[20]

### *A: The Middle Tower*

Constructed in 1275–81 as part of Edward I's new western entrance to the Tower, the Middle Tower was the first of the Tower of London's great gatehouses passed through by the visitor.[21] A drawbridge gave access from the Lion Tower, while portcullises could be dropped at either end of the gate passage to close the entrance way between the two great cylindrical towers. In the gateway itself a door in each tower gives access to the rooms within them, the northern tower housing the staircase leading to the upper rooms — which were substantially rebuilt in the eighteenth century. Provided with fireplaces and a garderobe, the rooms within the Middle Tower formed a discrete lodging, which in the early sixteenth century belonged to the Usher of the Exchange. Later in the century the lodging belonged to the Porter of the Mint, who was no doubt assigned such commanding lodgings as he was responsible for keeping gate for all the Mint's incomings and outgoings.[22] In this period the Tower was often known, confusingly, as the Martin Tower (or 'Saint Martin's Tower'), though the Haiward and Gascoyne plan uses the modern nomenclature.[23] The various repairs to the building proposed in 1532 were not effected; and though in the report on the state of the Tower made at the beginning of Queen Elizabeth's reign the poor repair of the leads over this gatehouse was singled out for particular mention,[24] the only accounts for repairs to the building in the whole reign were for bricking up windows in the lower room.[25]

### *B: The Tower at the Gate* — BYWARD TOWER

The final part of the great defensive entrance to the Tower built between 1275 and 1281 by Edward I, the Byward Tower — like the Middle — was equipped with a gate, two portcullises and a drawbridge.[26]

Although the Byward Tower was not the first gateway through which visitors to the Tower passed, it was 'the most principal',[27] and has, therefore, since the early sixteenth century at least, been the place where the warders of the fortress were based. The estimate of works of 1532 calls the gatehouse 'the tower at the west gate the wardyng gate',[28] while Haiward and Gascoyne term it simply 'The Tower at the Gate'. By the end of the century its association with the warders had earned it the title of the 'Byward' gate.[29] This was the gate which was shut at night, indicating the closure of the Tower, any access to the castle thereafter being through the 'little wycket' which was itself to be guarded by two warders.[30]

In 1548 a barrel of gunpowder in 'the round bulwarke, betwixt the west gate and the Posterne, or drawbridge, called the warders gate' exploded; the blast killed a French prisoner detained there and the tower itself was 'thrown downe'. This must have been the southern tower of the Byward gatehouse which shows signs of substantial internal re-facing in the Tudor period — presumably the result of the tower being 'new builded' after the explosion. The Under Porter of the Tower, who was responsible for the building, was subsequently imprisoned for keeping both gunpowder and prisoners in such an inappropriate place.[31]

The first-floor chamber of the Byward Tower, which still retains some of its extraordinary painted decoration of *c.* 1400, was clearly a high-status room in the Middle Ages. However, by the mid-seventeenth century the 'Byward or Round Tower over the Byward gates' was designated 'al ward$^{r}$s lodging';[32] the construction of a Tudor fireplace on the south wall, partly destroying the painted scene, might suggest its use as a warder's lodging dates from that period. It may be that this first-floor room was part of the lodgings of the Gentleman Porter, the chief officer of the Yeoman Warders. The Deputy Porter's lodgings were almost certainly in the Byward gate area, as is shown by an order to move the watch post from its usual position to the Iron Gate when his lodging became infected with the plague in July 1576.[33] As the Gentleman Porter was categorically commanded to 'sarve in parson and nott p[er] deputam',[34] it may well be that the deputy he did appoint inhabited part or all of his lodgings. If the Gentleman Porter's lodging was indeed in the Byward Tower, then the provision of new stairs for it in 1596–7[35] may be related to the moving of the entrance to the spiral staircase from within the lower chamber of the Byward Tower to the back of the gatehouse which took place in this period.[36]

The Haiward and Gascoyne survey shows a cluster of buildings adjoining the Byward Tower. To the north the survey shows the roof of a building running east-west between the Bell and Byward, in the position of the later Stone Kitchen alehouse. Though the Stone Kitchen is only known to have operated here from the late seventeenth century,[37] Sir John Peyton complained in 1597 that he had to endure 'a Comon Brewhouse, and Backhouse to bee kept w$^{th}$in y$^{e}$ mint', and the position of this building close by the Mint offices might suggest it was already a tavern in his day.[38] To the east of the Byward Tower is shown a gabled building overlooking the moat; the function of this building is not known, though its position makes it possible that, like the 'warder's hall' shown here in the late seventeenth century, it was used by the warders in some way.

The triangular-fronted turret projecting to the south of the Byward Tower, probably an addition of the late fifteenth century, was constructed to protect the postern entrance to the Tower from the wharf; to this end it was equipped with gun embrasures. In the sixteenth century the postern was still a functioning secondary entrance to the Tower, reached via a drawbridge from the wharf,[39] and it was probably by this entrance that Princess Elizabeth entered the fortress as a prisoner on 18 March 1554.[40] The bridge leading to the Byward gate was shored up in 1533, as a temporary measure, but it was apparently not until 1596–7 that it was replaced by a new bridge.[41]

## LEGGE'S MOUNT

The large semicircular bastion on the north-west corner of the outer curtain wall owes its current name to George Legge, Master-General of the Ordnance 1682–9. It seems to have been without a name in the sixteenth century and is certainly unlabelled on the Haiward and Gascoyne survey. The structure was built by Edward I as part of his new outer curtain wall and was raised in height soon afterwards, as was the wall itself. Before being raised further to its present height in the late seventeenth century, to house two tiers of guns, the bastion was, therefore, of much the same height as the curtain walls on either side.[42]

By the early sixteenth century the Mint was well established in the space between the two curtain walls at the north of the Tower, and the north-west bastion — called 'the bulwark of bryck & stone' — was described as that which 'stondith behynde the mynt'.[43] Excavations in the 1970s revealed the remains of a brick building provided with a furnace which stood against the inner face of the bastion, within which were found dozens of objects connected to the work of the Mint. The results of the excavation suggested that the area within Legge's Mount was used for assaying, that is, the testing of coinage to discover its silver or gold content. It was calculated that the furnace was probably active for the last time between 1530 and 1560.[44] It may be that the abandonment of the furnace there was a result of concerns about the strength of the defences of the fortress: in March 1559 it was recommended that the 'bulwerke in the mynte' should have 'a brycke or stone wall made on the insyde therof and to be filled full with earthe bothe for the strength of the place and also as it is it leyth unseamely for suche an house'.[45] However, the Haiward and Gascoyne plan clearly shows two buildings standing within the area of the bastion, indicating this scheme was not implemented.

One of the great northern bastions, perhaps Legge's Mount, was included in the estimate of 1564 for new platforms for guns, which mentions one demi-culverin 'In the Mint ... in the great Bulwark there'.[46]

### *Mount* — BRASS MOUNT

Like that at the north-west corner, the bastion at the north-east was built as part of Edward I's extension of the defences of the Tower. However, it seems that in the first instance the walls of the outer curtain wall met at the north-east corner without any bastion at the join and that the Brass Mount, with its firing gallery in the thickness of the walls, was only added when the outer curtain wall was heightened later in the reign.[47] By the end of the sixteenth century the Brass Mount was closed at the rear, and seems not to have been used by the Mint in the way Legge's Mount was; indeed, it appears that the Brass Mount functioned simply as a defensive bastion in this period, unlike many of the other medieval defensive constructions which had been commandeered by one or other of the departments of state operating within the Tower. The description of it as the 'green Mount' in 1641 suggests the area within it had become grassed over, or even that the walls themselves had become covered in vegetation.[48]

### *O: The Tower leading to ye Irongate* — DEVELIN TOWER

There is no consensus about the date of the building shown at the southern tip of the outer curtain wall on Haiward and Gascoyne's survey. It may have been the work of Edward I in the 1270s, or perhaps the fourteenth-century successor to Edward I's original building.[49] What is certain is that since the Tudor period the building has been significantly altered, by partial rebuilding in the late seventeenth century and a variety of works since.

The estimate of 1532 describes the building now known as the Develin Tower as the 'Gallyman' tower,[50] but this does not seem to have been a very long-lived name. Haiward and Gascoyne call the building simply 'The Tower leading to ye Irongate', suggesting that it was actually a gatehouse giving access to the little-used eastern entrance to the Tower. The vulnerable position of the Develin Tower, on the outer curtain wall adjoining a bridge across the moat, would have made it unsuitable for housing prisoners and there is no evidence any were kept here in this period. Instead, the Tower functioned, by the 1640s at least, as a warder's lodging, and it may be that 'Gallyman' was a resident of the early Tudor period.[51]

### *P: The Tower above Irongate* — IRON GATE

The date of the construction of the Iron Gate Tower, across the moat from the Develin Tower, is unclear. It is not at all certain that it was part of Edward I's work and might, instead, have been erected during the building campaign of the 1330s, or even at the end of the fourteenth century when the wharf was finally extended to meet the riverbank east of the castle.[52]

The Iron Gate gave access to the fortress from the east, but was apparently seldom used in the sixteenth century.[53] In 1532 'The great Towr at the Easte ende of the utter gate' was to have new roofs and floors;[54] although the gates of the gatehouse were replaced in the autumn of 1535 nothing more was done there until the following year, and then not the repairs envisaged in 1532.[55] In February 1536 the bridge which ran between the Iron Gate Tower and the Develin Tower was examined and found to 'require repair',[56] and as a result during the following winter both the ironwork and timber of the drawbridge were replaced.[57] The stonework of the building was not repaired at this time and the structure suffered as a result: in around 1570 it was reported that 'the wall of the Iron gate in greate decay both of stone and Iron worke'.[58] This state of affairs was allowed to continue until July 1576, when there was an outbreak of plague in a building at the Byward Tower entrance, and it was ordered that the main ward-house should be at the Iron Gate instead. To make this possible, the Lieutenant was to carry out immediate repairs as 'the bridge is in decaye'.[59]

The new arrangement was clearly temporary and the western entrance was soon back in operation. If the Lieutenant did carry out repairs to the bridge in 1576 they were no doubt of a cursory nature and it was not until the 1590s that the Iron Gate entrance and bridge were properly repaired: in 1592–3 new gates were installed,[60] while in the following year the drawbridge was replaced and the overdue works were carried out on the stonework 'to make the drawe bridge to falle currant'.[61] Despite these improvements, the Iron Gate entrance continued to be infrequently used; in the last years of Elizabeth's reign John Stow wrote of the tower: 'towards the East is a great and strong gate, commonly called the Iron gate, but not usually opened'.[62] By the 1640s disuse had taken its toll and the 'Iron Gate Towr' was described simply as 'An old Ruynous place towards St Katherins'.[63]

### *N: Well Tower*

The Well Tower was probably built at the same time as the outer curtain wall, on which it lies, in the reign of Edward I,[64] and may owe its name to the stone-lined chutes which enabled water from the river to be drawn from within the building.[65]

A wall ran north from the Well Tower to the Salt Tower, as can be seen on the Haiward and Gascoyne survey, the gateway through which would have given access to Water Lane from the Iron Gate entrance.[66] However, the infrequency of the use of the Iron Gate in the sixteenth century is testified to by the fact that the area of the Outer Ward between this wall and the Lanthorn Tower was used as a royal garden throughout the Tudor period. In Henry VIII's reign it was designated the queen's garden, and in Elizabeth's — in the absence of a consort — the privy garden.[67] The Well Tower itself comprises two storeys and a staircase turret at the north-east corner; the 1532 estimate recommended that the floors in both the tower and the turret be replaced, though this seems not to have happened,[68] instead a new window was made in the building.[69] The graffiti in the upper chamber shows that the tower was being used to house prisoners from the 1580s at least,[70] and it may be that the bricking-up of a window in 1593–4, and the mending of the chimney there in the 1590s, were measures intended to make the building more suitable for this purpose.[71] Certainly by 1641 the tower was categorically described as 'A prison lodging'.[72]

### *Q: The Cradle Tower*

Built by Edward III between 1348 and 1355, the Cradle Tower formed a new entrance to the Tower of London from the River Thames. Some ten years previously a gateway was apparently made in the inner curtain wall to its north (later incorporated into the long gallery shown on the 1597 survey), thus the Cradle Tower would have given direct access from the water to the royal apartments, which by this time were clustered around the Lanthorn Tower.[73] With the extension of the wharf to St Katharine's in the 1390s the Cradle Tower was cut off from the river and instead only gave access to the moat.

By the end of the sixteenth century the Cradle Tower was certainly serving as a prison lodging. It was here that John Arden was imprisoned for over a decade until his daring escape in the company of the Catholic priest, John Gerard, in 1597.[74] As was the case with many of those imprisoned in the mural towers, John Arden — despite having been sentenced to death — was allowed to take the air on the leads over his lodging on a daily basis. Although the outside door was barred by Arden's warder, it seems the door to the leads was usually left open for the prisoner to wander there as he pleased, the width of the moat between the Cradle Tower and the wharf no doubt being considered sufficient to preclude any possibility of escape.[75] John Arden was probably kept in the upper storey of the Cradle Tower; this no longer exists, having been taken down in 1776 and then reconstructed in the late 1870s.

It seems as though the Cradle Tower was still occasionally used as a watergate until the end of the century; Stow describes the tower as 'a small Posterne with a draw bridge, seldome letten downe but for the receipt of som great persons, prisoners'.[76] The way in which the drawbridge operated is unclear, but perhaps was lowered to form a jetty of some sort.

### *V: S^t^ Thomas Tower*

St Thomas's Tower was built between 1275 and 1281 as the entrance to the Tower from the river, giving access to the Outer Ward from the Thames through the new outer curtain wall. Over the basin the building contained a new hall and chamber, lavishly fitted out, possibly for the accommodation of the king. By the late fourteenth century the royal apartments centred on the Lanthorn Tower and the rooms around the Wakefield Tower had been converted for other uses. The Wakefield Tower itself was commandeered by the Wardrobe, while by 1325 St Thomas's Tower was being used to lodge important members of the court rather than the king himself and was shortly afterwards racked out as an armoury.[77]

In June 1532 an indenture was drawn up between Thomas Cromwell and James Nedeham for the 'reëdifying of St Thomas's Tower', which was to consist primarily in the renewal of the timber work and roof of the upper storey.[78] It is interesting that this was dealt with separately from the great body of works outlined in the estimate of 1532, which omits any mention of repairs to St Thomas's Tower. The works were largely carried out between June and September 1532 and included removing the old timber frame of the lodging as it was and replacing it,[79] providing a new roof and floors,[80] and installing two stone pillars under the medieval stone arch.[81] In the autumn of 1532 the basin was given new gates and stairs[82] and the roof was re-leaded.[83] The new roof was perhaps intended to bear the weight of cannon, and certainly in 1564 two falcons and one falconet were mounted on the leads there.[84]

The works continued in the spring of 1533 at which time the interior of the rebuilt lodging was given attention: chimneys were repaired, and partitions were erected to form two lodgings.[85] These were assigned to the most important officials involved in the coronation of Anne Boleyn: the Lord Great Chamberlain, the Earl of Oxford, who was the official in charge of the coronation and who carried the crown in the procession to Westminster Abbey, and the Lord Chamberlain of the Household, Lord Sandys, who was responsible for all the ceremonies which took place within the royal palaces.[86] Thus, though St Thomas's Tower was no longer part of the king's lodgings, it provided accommodation for his most senior household officials.

After the coronation of Queen Anne in 1533, the Lord Chamberlain and Lord Great Chamberlain would no longer have required accommodation at the Tower as Henry VIII's court never stayed there again. However, the rooms in St Thomas's Tower continued to function as a lodging. In March 1554 Edward Courtenay, who had been implicated in Wyatt's rebellion, was moved to St Thomas's Tower from the Bell Tower. This is the only reference this author has found to the lodging over the watergate being used as a prison and should be treated as an exception, springing perhaps from the combination of the great pressure on space at the Tower in the early months of 1554 and Courtenay's own very high status.[87] The position of St Thomas's Tower, straddling the moat, must have made it relatively easy to escape from and, therefore, unsuitable as a prison. Perhaps as a result of the rarity of royal visits to the Tower in the reign of Elizabeth I, the lodgings over the watergate were not kept free for some great court officer but were assigned instead to officials of the Tower.[88] At some point in the sixteenth or early seventeenth century St Thomas's Tower was home to the King's fletchers, and by 1641 was assigned to warders.[89]

Perhaps surprisingly, the romantic epithet of 'Traitors' Gate' for St Thomas's Tower has been in use since the early seventeenth century: in 1611 the building was described as 'the Bridg called Traitors staires'.[90] As the Tower of London was used to incarcerate those accused of the most serious crimes, and as St Thomas's Tower was the river entrance to it, there is nothing remarkable about the association of the two. There is, though, nothing to suggest that those accused of treason were particularly brought through the watergate. Indeed one of the most famous prisoners of the Tower associated with 'Traitors' Gate', Princess Elizabeth, was actually 'taken in at the drawebridge' — probably the Byward postern — and not at St Thomas's Tower at all.[91]

### *The Mint*

A branch of the Royal Mint seems to have been established within the Tower in the late 1270s. The location of its premises at this time is not clear, but the 400-foot building which the Warden of the Mint was instructed to erect in 1300 to house thirty new furnaces was very likely in the Outer Ward between the two principal curtain walls.[92] By the early sixteenth century a whole assortment of Mint buildings had grown up in the Tower, to which more were added in 1514, when the Prior of St Bartholomew's was paid for 'new making and transposing storehouses and coining houses in the Tower'.[93]

The coinage reforms of 1526 increased the Mint's work significantly and as a result its buildings received considerable attention. Order was made for the 'old Mint houses in the farther Mint yard' to be emptied of the ordnance which had come to be stored there and to be repaired to make room for the foreign coiners to work.[94] A new house was constructed for the shearing of gold — that is the slicing of long bars of gold into the thin disks which were to become individual coins — and windows were mended.[95] The receipt house was taken down and rebuilt.[96] Many, if not all, of these buildings were located within the Outer Ward on the east, north and west of the castle: archaeological evidence of Mint activity has been found in what is now known as Legge's Mount (see above), and this is supported by the documentary material.[97]

Following the drastic coinage debasement of the 1540s and 1550s, the decision was taken in 1559 to withdraw from circulation what remained of Henry VIII and Edward VI's base silver coin. This was a huge, one-off operation, in preparation for which there was a great spurt of building activity at the Tower of London, which was, by now, home to the only mint in England. In 1560–1 three new mint buildings came into action. Two of these were refining houses, one constructed somewhere within the Inmost Ward for the German refiners who had won the commission to purify the withdrawn coin, and the other outside the walls of the fortress within the Queen's storehouse at East Smithfield.[98] The process of re-coining took several years, after which it seems likely these two refining houses ceased to be part of the Mint. The third new building was called simply the 'new upper mint within the Tower'. The upper mint was the branch of the Mint responsible for the re-coining of the base money; it had a separate staff and under-treasurer during the years of re-coinage.[99] Its new building 'within the Tower' contained a refining house, a melting house and an annealing house, was constructed largely of timber and brick and had a tiled roof.[100] The location of the new upper mint is unclear;[101] however, when the tiled roof over the 'upper melting house' was replaced in 1601–2 it was described as being 'under the Mounte', which would indicate that the upper mint was at the northern end of the Outer Ward adjoining either the north-east or north-west bastion.[102]

Further buildings were added in the course of Elizabeth's reign: in 1565–7 a new blanching house (where coinage was whitened by treatment with acid) was erected,[103] while in 1584–5 repairs were carried out to a Mint building, including 'woorkeinge upon postes and railes for the leaden roofe'.[104] This must have been the single-storey building to the west of the Brass Mount, which the Haiward and Gascoyne survey shows topped with a lead roof and a line of posts and rails. As this seems to have been the only substantial lead roofed building in the Mint, it was probably here that the gun platforms were to be placed in 1564.[105]

In the mid-1580s the roof of the 'Mill mint' was also repaired; this may have been where the mill or 'engyne' used by Frenchman Eloye Mestrell to mint coins mechanically, had been housed.[106] The Mint was one of the attractions of the Tower shown to important visitors.[107] Queen Elizabeth herself visited in 1561, an occasion for which nineteen loads of gravel were ordered to lay the paths,[108] and it is possible it was Mestrell's new machine that she came to see. The Warden of the Mint complained of the dangers posed by the hordes flocking to look at Mestrell's engine, which was kept in a building that 'adioynithe next to the lodginge of many prisoners in the tower...'.[109]

In 1585–6 an office with a large bay window was erected at the 'further end of the mynte', which was perhaps one of the houses shown to the north of the Byward Tower in the 1597 survey. By the 1580s, if not well before, Mint accommodation stretched right round the Outer Ward to the Salt Tower.[110] The Haiward and Gascoyne survey certainly shows long buildings reaching round three sides of the Outer Ward, many — if not all — of which must have been part of the Mint. It also shows a dotted line running right round the Outer Ward, which perhaps indicated the extent of the Mint's jurisdiction within the Tower.[111]

### *C: The Bell Tower*

Datable on structural grounds to the late twelfth or early thirteenth centuries, the Bell Tower is likely to have been built for Richard I by his chief minister, William Longchamp, or perhaps under King John in the early thirteenth century. When first built it formed the south-western corner of the fortress, and would have been lapped by the River Thames.[112] Subsequent refortification of the Tower left the Bell Tower on the corner of the inner curtain wall; a wall pierced by a gate ran south from it to the outer curtain wall,[113] while by the end of the seventeenth century the Stone Kitchen tavern operated in a building which ran between the Byward and Bell towers, and the roof of a building in just this location is shown on the Haiward and Gascoyne survey.

Access into the building as a whole was through the Lieutenant's lodgings, which the Haiward and Gascoyne plan show tucked into the corner of the Ward. The current Queen's House was built to house the Lieutenant in 1540, but its predecessor clearly stood in the same position.[114] The construction of the new lodgings must have involved alterations in the access arrangements for the Bell Tower, and it may be that the brickwork on the ground floor — perhaps closing access to the wall passage in the curtain wall to the north — dates from this time.[115] The upper and lower chambers of the Bell Tower do not connect internally today but reference to the mending of 'vyces' in the 1532 estimate implies internal connection at that date.[116]

It was probably this proximity to the lodgings of the Lieutenant, who was responsible for the prisoners in the Tower, which caused the Bell Tower to be used to house powerful and politically sensitive detainees.[117] It has for some time been held that Thomas More was housed in the lower chamber. There is no contemporary proof of this statement, but — nevertheless — it is likely that More was kept somewhere where he could be closely watched, and references in More's letters to his being taken from his cell along a gallery to see the Lieutenant do suggest his lodging adjoined the Queen's House.[118] Another supposed inhabitant, Princess Elizabeth, actually lodged in the royal apartments, not the Bell Tower.[119]

Among those who were held here was John Fisher, Bishop of Rochester; Fisher was apparently kept on the upper floor of the tower and was so weak that on the day of his execution he could barely manage to descend the stairs.[120] Edward Courtenay was lodged in the Bell Tower for a month or so in early 1554 before being moved to St Thomas's Tower[121] while both Robert and Guildford Dudley were given the liberty to walk on the leads over the Bell Tower in October 1553.[122] The bell cote and bell over the tower today are seventeenth century but their predecessors were presumably in much the same position — this was doubtless the function of the little structure shown on the roof on the 1597 survey.[123] The bell was rung at five o'clock as 'a signal for all to leave unless they want to have the gates shut on them'.[124]

### *D: Buecamp Tower* — BEAUCHAMP TOWER

In 1281, having completed the new entrance to the fortress in the south-west corner, Edward I replaced his father's ill-fated western entrance with the imposing Beauchamp Tower. Much of the western curtain wall on either side was reconstructed at the same time.[125]

During the Tudor period the Beauchamp Tower was used frequently, if not constantly, as a prison lodging. The extraordinary number of inscriptions on the walls of the building is a testament to the sheer number of people incarcerated here at this time.[126] Three floors high, there was enough room in the

Beauchamp Tower to accommodate several detainees at once, though the concentration of inscriptions on the middle storey suggests this was the most frequently used.

A list of prisoners in the Tower dated 6 July 1535 records seven men 'In Becham Tower': three priests, three coiners and one 'squire'.[127] Prisoners were often moved around the fortress to make best use of the limited and variable accommodation. The buildings on Tower Green, west of the White Tower in the Inner Ward, seem to have been among the most desirable.[128] While the priest Thomas Abell was one of the seven men kept in the Beauchamp Tower in 1535, two years later he was being held elsewhere in the castle; when he petitioned Thomas Cromwell to have his conditions improved, he asked to be allowed to take mass in the Chapel and 'to lie in some house upon the Green'.[129] Some of the many members of the Dudley family, imprisoned by Mary I after the collapse of Lady Jane Grey's bid for the throne, were detained in the Beauchamp Tower, as is demonstrated by the graffiti on the middle and ground floors. In September 1553 two of the Dudley brothers were granted the freedom to walk on the roof over the building.[130]

Depending on demands of space, the Beauchamp Tower might hold several prisoners of middling status, or one of high status. In 1572 three men were lodged in the tower, two of whom had been implicated in the Ridolfi Plot.[131] The first Earl of Arundel was lodged there for some, at least, of his decade at the Tower;[132] repairs were carried out for him in 1594–5 at which time the fireplaces were repaired and the decaying floors paved with brick.[133] The lead over the roof had been replaced in 1591–2.[134] From 1603 the Beauchamp Tower was assigned to Henry Brooke, Lord Cobham, imprisoned for conspiring against the succession of James I. Shortly before Cobham's incarceration there the Beauchamp Tower had been repaired again: the wall which ran south to the Lieutenant's lodgings received attention, while the 'upper roome' was whitewashed.[135] Cobham remained a prisoner until his death some sixteen years later, becoming so closely associated with the building in which he was held that in the 1640s it was still alternatively known as 'Cobham Tower'.[136]

### *E: Devilin Tower* — DEVEREUX TOWER

The substantial angle tower now known as the Devereux Tower was built by Henry III between the last years of the 1230s and first of the 1240s. The tower formed the north-west corner of the new curtain wall which ran round the three landward sides of the castle to the Lanthorn Tower.[137] Standing two storeys high with two staircase turrets, a second floor was only inserted into the upper storey of the building in the eighteenth century.

By the 1530s the building was known as 'Robin the Devil's Tower', which, it has been suggested, was in reference to William the Conqueror's father, who was known as Robert 'le Diable'.[138] In the estimate of 1532 significant works were recommended to the building. The spiral staircases were to be repaired with Caen stone, while the top seven feet of the walls of the tower were apparently to be taken down and reconstructed.[139] In the works which were in fact carried out in the following year or so the timber in the building was replaced,[140] bricklayers were employed in 'crestyng & mendyng' it,[141] while plumbers replaced the lead on the roof.[142] One of the final things done to the building at this time was 'the hythenyng of the flower w[th] brycke Ragstone and chalk',[143] this could refer to either the lower or upper storey as the unusual vaulted basement could have supported a stone floor above.

It is unclear what the Devereux Tower was used for during the sixteenth century. Although the Marquis of Northampton watched the execution of Guildford Dudley on Tower Hill, on 13 February 1554, from the roof of the building, there is nothing to suggest it was used as a prison lodging.[144] The building is sometimes said to owe its modern name to the incarceration there of Robert Devereux, Earl of Essex, in 1601, but there is no real evidence for this. On a plan of 1682 the building was called the 'Deverin' Tower, which would suggest the name was gradually corrupted from 'Devil' or 'Develin' to 'Devereux' over the years rather than suddenly changed.[145]

By the 1550s the tower was certainly provided with roof-top ordnance, which was fired on the City during Wyatt's rebellion.[146] The Haiward and Gascoyne survey shows the building to have been surrounded by a swarm of buildings in the Inner Ward, many — if not all — of which belonged to the Ordnance Office,[147] and it may be that the Devereux Tower too was used by that department.[148]

### *F: Flint Tower*

The building of this name which stands on the northern section of the inner curtain wall today is not that shown on the Haiward and Gascoyne survey. The current building was erected in about 1800 after its predecessor 'having fallen greatly into decay' was 'taken down nearly to the ground'.[149] The original tower — which is that shown on the Haiward and Gascoyne survey — was one of the nine towers erected by Henry III along the new curtain wall in the late 1230s and early 1240s.[150]

The great building estimate of 1532 calls the Flint Tower 'Bowear's' tower — a name which, on the 1597 survey, and ever since has been applied to its eastern neighbour.[151] The estimate recommended, among other things, that the two turrets of this tower be reconstructed, but there is no sign in the accounts of the works which followed of this being done.

Almost nothing is known about the function of the Flint Tower in the Tudor period. After the construction of the Ordnance storehouses of 1545–7 access to it from the Inner Ward would appear to have been through these storehouses, and it would, therefore, seem likely it was used by the Ordnance Office, though there is no direct evidence for this in the sixteenth century. The estimate of 1564 includes provision for a gun platform over the leads of the Flint Tower, to be 27 foot by 23 foot and to carry two falcons.[152] These guns must have been important for the defence of the Tower against any approach from Tower Hill, which as the apprentices' riot of 1595 showed, was an area in which violent confrontation could easily flare up. The enigmatic description of what were probably the Flint and Bowyer Towers as 'Two london Towers behinde ye ordnce office' in 1641 may refer to their role in protecting the fortress from any approach from the landward side.[153]

### *G: Bowyar Tower* — BOWYER TOWER

The Bowyer Tower stands on the line of the Roman wall which until the reign of Henry III formed the eastern boundary of the fortress. The building shown on the Haiward and Gascoyne survey, of which only the lower storey remains today, was constructed in *c.* 1239–41; the upper storey of the building had, by 1820, already been rebuilt in brick.[154]

The tower was called 'Burbedge' tower in 1532 when, like its neighbour the Flint, it was recommended that its turret be rebuilt and its stonework repaired.[155] The plumbers' account for work to the roof of the building in the later part of the year refers to windlasses, which were perhaps for hoisting ordnance on to the leads.[156] In 1564 a platform 31 foot by 23 foot was included in an estimate for new gun platforms for the Tower, intended, in this case, to carry one falcon and one robinet.[157]

Since the early nineteenth century, at least, the Bowyer Tower has been associated with the incarceration of George, Duke of Clarence in 1478, and his subsequent demise in the apocryphal butt of malmsey wine. As was pointed out as early as the 1820s, in the first serious history of the Tower of London, this is 'unsupported by any historical evidence'.[158] There is, in fact, no evidence for the Bowyer Tower being used as a prison lodging during the sixteenth century, and both its name and location make it more likely that the tower was used by the institutions responsible for military supplies operating within the Tower of London.

### *H: Brick Tower*

Like its neighbours along the north and east stretches of the inner curtain wall, the tower known since the sixteenth century as the Brick Tower was presumably constructed as part of Henry III's extension and improvement of the Tower's defences. The Brick Tower was one of the few parts of the mural defences which were substantially rebuilt in the Tudor period. In 1513 several sums of money were allowed to the Lieutenant of the Tower and the Master of the Ordnance, for work to 'the tower at the back of the ordnance house in the Tower of London'.[159] That this was the Brick Tower is indicated by the great estimate for works of 1532; this prescribes considerable repairs for all the towers along the north inner curtain wall except the Brick Tower, which is described as 'The bryck tower the maister of thordynance lodging new repayrede w[t] bryck safe at the foundacion'.[160]

The building was by the 1820s 'altogether in a state of decay' and was subsequently rebuilt so that the structure which bears this name today is entirely nineteenth-century. Before the building was demolished the distinguished Tower historian John Bayley remarked that the lower storey 'corresponds with that of' the Bowyer Tower, and that the upper was built of brick. This would indicate, therefore, that the rebuilding of 1513 left the lower storey largely intact and saw the upper floor only reconstructed in brick.[161]

By the 1530s the building was the residence of the Master of the Ordnance, a function it continued to perform throughout the century, being described in 1641 as 'By y[e] Armory, the Ma[r] of y[e] Ordnce lordgeings'.[162] However, though the building may have been designated as such, as was the case with many of the greatest officers who had lodgings in the Tower of London, the Master of the Ordnance did not often reside there. In these circumstances the Lieutenant of the Tower clearly took advantage of the vacant space and assigned the lodging to someone else. In October 1551 the Privy Council specifically ordered the Lieutenant of the Tower, Arthur Darcy, to 'remove such as be lodged within the lodging of our ... Master of our Ordinaunce and see the same voyded and left free for the sayd Master of our Ordinanunce to repayre unto at all tymes requisite'.[163]

### *I: Martin Tower*

The Martin Tower, built in the late 1230s or early 1240s by Henry III, stands at the point at which the new curtain wall which runs north from the Salt Tower, turned north-westwards. The two-storeyed tower remains today, with its basement chamber intact (originally vaulted), though the upper chamber was divided into two levels by the insertion of a floor in the late seventeenth century.

In the works estimate of 1532 it was recommended that the 'tower at theaste ende', as the Martin Tower was called,[164] have its staircases re-made, a new timber floor inserted and the timber of the roofs of the two turrets replaced. None of these things are recorded in the accounts for the works which followed.[165] By the end of the sixteenth century the building was clearly being used to house prisoners: much of the dated graffiti on the walls is from the last decades of the sixteenth and first of the seventeenth centuries, while in 1641 it is described as 'Martin Tower Over against the green Mount neare Mr Sherburns house a prison lodging'.[166] The repairs to the building of 1596/7, which included boarding the ground floor and fixing iron bars in the windows, were doubtless intended to make it better equipped to hold prisoners.[167]

### *K: Constable Tower*

The Constable Tower was built by Henry III in *c.* 1239–41 and considerably altered in the nineteenth century.[168] Towards the end of the reign of Elizabeth I the tower was used to house prisoners; one of the problems of using crumbling medieval towers in this way is shown by an account of 1594–5 for 'makinge up a windowe in Constable Tower, and mendeinge that a prisoner digged out'.[169] In the last years of the century considerable repairs were carried out to the Constable Tower: the stairs leading to the tower were cased with boards and a wooden roof constructed 'to keepe the weather from them',[170] the top of the chimney shaft was taken down and rebuilt,[171] gutters were replaced[172] and the stairs leading on to the leads were repaired.[173] Repairs of this nature, which would have made the building considerably more comfortable, suggest the Constable Tower was being prepared to house someone of importance, whether a prisoner or not. Certainly by 1641, though, the tower could be designated 'a prison lodging'.[174]

The nature of the connection between the Constable Tower and the lodgings of the Constable of the Tower is difficult to understand. No constables of the Tower were appointed until the end of Elizabeth's reign, and the report made on the state of the Tower in 1559 specifies that 'the lodging called the Constables house must be repayred or ells it is lyke wise in daunger to fall, for the fundation therof fayleth'.[175] The Constable's house is only once mentioned in any detail in the Elizabethan building accounts (in 1600–1) and it is in a way which implied it was connected to the tower of the same name: 'joyntinge and settinge upp of a newe border for a chymney in the Lorde highe Constables dyneinge chamber mending the windowes there takinge downe the upper parte of staires goeing upp to the Leades over Constables Tower'.[176] Though the evidence is slim, it may just be that the Constable's lodgings were in one of the houses which adjoined the Constable Tower, buildings which in the following century were certainly assigned to some of the most important residents of the Tower of London.[177] Substantial works were done to one of these buildings in 1602–3, a year after the repairs to the Constable's dining room: these included building a new storey on 'the great house adjoininge to the Constable Tower', and re-flooring 'in the greate Chamber of the same house'.[178]

### *L: Broad Arrow Tower*

The Broad Arrow Tower was constructed by Henry III in the late 1230s or early 1240s, forming part of the wall which marked the eastern boundary of the newly enlarged fortress. The building originally comprised two storeys: the current low third storey being created by the insertion of a floor towards the end of the nineteenth century.[179]

Like the Martin and Constable towers, the Broad Arrow was, in the works estimate of 1532, considered to require general repairs to the stonework and staircases. While the proposed repairs to the first two were never carried out, the Broad Arrow Tower actually received more attention than was initially recommended. In the later months of 1532 plumbers re-laid the leads,[180] bricklayers mended the chimney and roughcast the exterior of the tower,[181] while carpenters worked on the roof of the tower and turrets, new boarded the floors and — it seems — installed an altar into one of the turrets.[182] As the north turret contains a staircase, the altar was presumably placed in the tiny top floor room of the southern turret, accessible only from the leads. The existence of what seems to have been a small oratory in the Broad Arrow Tower would indicate that it was at this time a lodging of some importance. It may be that it was to be used to house one of the many high-ranking courtiers who stayed in the Tower with the King and Queen in the days before Anne Boleyn's coronation on 1 June 1533.

Despite the Broad Arrow's apparent use as a high status lodging in the 1530s, graffiti in the tower shows that by the 1550s, at the latest, prisoners were being accommodated there. Among these were Giovanni Battista Castiglione held for questioning by Queen

Mary in 1556. From this time onwards, the Broad Arrow Tower continued to served as a prison and in 1641 was described as 'upon y$^{e}$ wall by y$^{e}$ Kings Garden a prison lodging'.[183] Like the Constable Tower, the Broad Arrow was repaired in the late 1590s — the stairs into the tower also being covered by a timber roof to keep them dry,[184] though it is unclear whether this was done to prepare the building for a particular inhabitant.

### *M: Salt Tower*

The Salt Tower stands at the south-eastern corner of the new curtain wall built by Henry III. The building originally comprised three storeys: the current third floor being a relatively modern insertion into the upper chamber. By the early Tudor period the tower was usually known as 'Julius Caesar's tower'. The origin of this nomenclature is unknown. Certainly the Tower of London was, at this time, generally believed to have been founded by Caesar, but as the White Tower was clearly the oldest part of the fortress this was the building usually ascribed to him. By the end of the sixteenth century the Salt Tower was known by its modern name and the Haiward and Gascoyne plan gives 'Cæsar's' as an alternative name for the White Tower instead.

The Salt Tower was one of the buildings which underwent substantial works in the year preceding the coronation of Anne Boleyn. The carpenters took down the existing timber work and replaced the boards of both the first and second floors,[185] plumbers renewed the lead roof,[186] bricklayers mended the exterior and formed the foundations for one of the new floors,[187] freemasons repointed the tower and supplied new stone 'hewen to fynyshe it',[188] and roughcasters harled part of the exterior.[189] Given the position of the Salt Tower, adjoining the end of the King's gallery, and the extent of the works carried out in 1532–3, it seems likely that the tower was to be occupied by a member of the royal entourage during the pre-coronation celebrations.

The comfortable residential floors of the Salt Tower had, it seems, been used in 1296 to house one of the Tower's most important prisoners, John Balliol,[190] and continued to serve as a prison in the Tudor period. Extensive graffiti on the second and third storeys testifies to the hours wiled away by many Elizabethan detainees. Among these were Hugh Draper, accused of sorcery in 1560, whose elaborate astronomical clock can be seen carved into the wall in the first-floor chamber, and Sir John Perrot, former Lord Deputy of Ireland and supposed illegitimate son of Henry VIII, who was imprisoned here in 1590.[191] John Gerard, the Jesuit priest who made a dramatic escape from the roof of the Cradle Tower, was held here in 1597. His account of his imprisonment shows that the first and second floor chambers each functioned as a separate cell, with doors which could be secured with iron bars, an arrangement which presumably operated in many of the mural towers used to hold prisoners.[192] Straw was provided for Gerard to sleep on, but he was allowed to arrange for a mattress and linen and other items of comfort to be provided by his friends.[193] The Salt Tower's use as a prison continued well into the seventeenth century and it is one of the buildings designated 'a prison lodeging' in 1641.[194]

### *S: The Hall Tower* — WAKEFIELD TOWER

The Wakefield Tower was built by Henry III in about 1225, its first floor probably serving as the sovereign's own chamber; the building was apparently linked to Edward I's new watergate (St Thomas's Tower) at first-floor level later in the century. By the reign of Edward II the Wakefield Tower had become the domain of the Wardrobe, Edward III using the Lanthorn Tower and surrounding buildings as his inner-most chambers instead.[195]

In the early 1530s the Wakefield Tower and its adjoining chamber block were described as 'the tower and lodgyng of the kyngis Reco$^{r}$ds'. It may be that the collection of records of state kept in the Tower had been stored in the Wakefield since their removal from the White Tower in 1360, to make room for King John of France, but this is by no means certain. The lodging block immediately to the east of the Wakefield Tower seems to have been used partly as a record store and partly as a lodging or 'mansion', which with its adjoining garden was assigned to the King's bowmaker.[196] The Haiward and Gascoyne plan shows the doorway at the west end which presumably led into the record office, separated by a wall from the eastern part of the building, perhaps the bowmaker's house.

The Wakefield Tower received no attention in the great programme of works of the 1530s and indeed little was done to the building in the Tudor period as a whole. In 1579–80 107 shillings was spent on glazing in 'Thoffice of Recordes', at which time the 'murringe [walling] upp [of] sondrie lightes' was also recorded, as was joiner's work 'for two lathers' — presumably ladders to reach down the manuscripts.[197] At this time members of the public could, by appointment and for a fee, come to the Tower to consult the records.[198] The record office was, therefore, not simply a storehouse but must also have been provided with a reading room of some description for which reasonable lighting and easy access to the shelves were no doubt essential.

Although there seems to be no primary evidence of the placing of guns on the roof of the Wakefield Tower, the building is described as both the 'Artillery Tower' and 'Rownde Towre of the Artrie' during the fifteenth, sixteenth and early seventeenth centuries.[199] The implication being that the tower either carried guns, or perhaps that artillery was stored here during this period.

### *T: The Bloody Tower*

The precise dating of the medieval phases of the gatehouse known as the Bloody Tower is uncertain. The building is constructed of thirteenth- and fourteenth-century masonry and originally functioned as a water-gate fronting directly on to the river. The vault in the gate passage was inserted in 1360–2, and the tiles in the floor over it are probably also of this time.[200] It has been suggested that a reference to the 'chamber over the inner gate where the lord king was accustomed to sleep' in Edward III's reign refers to the Bloody Tower, but this is not the only building which fits that description.[201] The tower was originally provided with two portcullises; while that on the north side has long disappeared, a portcullis and winding gear survive on the southern side of the building.[202]

In the reign of Henry VIII the Bloody Tower was known by the rather less chilling name of the 'Garden Tower', in reference to the Lieutenant's garden which can be seen immediately to its north on the Haiward and Gascoyne survey. The name 'Bloody Tower' was certainly in use from the mid-1560s,[203] and as early as 1602 this was being interpreted as a reference to the supposed murder here of the sons of Edward IV.[204] Although there is no contemporary evidence for the 'princes in the Tower' being held in this building, the tower was frequently used as a prison for high-status detainees right through the sixteenth century.

Until the early seventeenth century, the Bloody Tower comprised only one storey above the vault and was generally used to house only one prisoner at a time. The proximity of the building to the Lieutenant's lodgings, and its relative comfort, ensured that it was used to house some of the Tower's most important prisoners.[205] In the summer of 1535 Thomas Fitzgerald, Earl of Kildare, was being held here,[206] while in Mary I's reign the Bloody Tower was the lodging of John Dudley, Duke of Northumberland (executed in August 1553), and three weeks later of Thomas Cranmer, Archbishop of Canterbury.[207]

In January 1572 Thomas Howard, fourth Duke of Norfolk, was convicted of treason for his involvement in the Ridolfi Plot. He seems to have been kept in the Bloody Tower and a letter from the Lieutenant of the Tower to the Queen's principal ministers describes the arrangements made for the security of so important a prisoner: 'the wyndowe at the duke his previe looketh into a lyttell yarde, the door wheof at the duke his cumyng I so nayled up, that no man can cum thether'; the other window looked into the Lieutenant's garden, but this was considered safe as the warders of the Tower often patrolled there.[208] Thus rather than simply boarding up the windows, which would have been much easier but less pleasant for the occupant, the Lieutenant ensured the security of the places which the prisoner could see or call to from the windows.

Shortly after the Haiward and Gascoyne plan was made, in 1605–6, a floor was inserted into the upper storey of the Bloody Tower 'to devide the roome into two Stories for S^r^ Walter Rawleigh' who had been imprisoned in the Tower of London since 1603.[209] Two new windows were made at the same time and the building slightly heightened.

### *The Lievetenants Lodgings* — QUEEN'S HOUSE

The building called the Lieutenant's lodgings on the Haiward and Gascoyne plan, and still standing today, was constructed in 1540 for Sir Edmund Walsingham, Lieutenant of the Tower of London at the time.[210] The new building replaced the previous Lieutenant's lodgings which stood on the same site,[211] and incorporated some of the medieval stonework of its predecessor.[212] The rebuilding was mooted for ten years before it actually happened: in 1532 'm^r^ lieutennte Lodging to be newe made' featured on the list of important works which had not yet begun.[213] By the autumn of 1533 it seems that it was accepted that this was not to happen imminently, tilers having been put to work on repairs 'ov^r^ m^r^ leuetennts hall and dyv^r^s other places of hys house'.[214] Only after much prompting, including the threat that the existing building would collapse at any moment, did works finally begin.[215]

The new building formed an L shape, tucked into the corner of the Inner Ward and backing on to the south and west inner curtain walls. The southern range of the building probably contained the hall in the second bay from the west, which until 1607 reached from the first floor to the roof, and the great kitchen in the eastern bay of the building.[216] The hall had a dais, re-made in 1593–4,[217] and a 'great stonne windowe' which was extensively repaired in 1602–3.[218] The latter is presumably the large gothic window which can be seen facing south over the inner curtain wall on the Haiward and Gascoyne plan.[219]

The Lieutenant of the Tower was responsible for the prisoners held at the castle and as a result his house was often used for their interrogation. John Gerard tells of passing through the hall to the dining hall for his 'examination',[220] the latter may perhaps have been the 'p[ar]lo$^{r}$ nexte the hall' of which the chimney was repaired in 1599–1600 and the windows in 1602–3.[221] It seems as though the principal rooms of the house were along the south side, the private being perhaps in the north-south range.[222]

The Lieutenant's kitchens received considerable attention in the 1590s, at which time his lodgings as a whole were reported to be 'in greate decaye'.[223] The pastry was re-floored and its two ovens were repaired,[224] the scullery was floored with brick, while the kitchen was paved in Purbeck stone,[225] and the hearths and ranges there were mended.[226] The kitchens were not just for the Lieutenant's benefit but also provided food for prisoners. The Privy Council sometimes permitted a few prisoners to eat at the Lieutenant's table as a special privilege, often extended to those who were unwell. Thus, in 1559 Thomas Watson, Bishop of Lincoln, who suffered from ague was permitted to 'come at suche tymes as he [the Lieutenant] by his discrecion shall thynke mete to his table'.[227] Twelve years later Watson was still permitted this privilege and was sharing it with three other prisoners in the Tower.[228] In 1591 Sir Nicholas White petitioned Burghley directly to be allowed access to the table 'being weak through long imprisonment'.[229] Therefore the Lieutenant's kitchens were providing for many more than the Lieutenant himself, indeed in 1599–1600 a bricklayer was at work in the Lieutenant's lodging on the 'Rannge in his Kitchen were the Prysoners meate in [*sic*] dreste' while in 1601–2 a new furnace was built specifically 'for boyling of Beife for the prisoners'.[230]

In addition to keeping a table for a few fortunate prisoners, the Lieutenant was sometimes required by the Privy Council to lodge important detainees within his house. Thus, in April 1552 the Lieutenant was both to examine the Countess of Sussex and to 'lodge the sayd Lady in his lodging'.[231] The elaborate graffiti in a room on the third floor reveals that the same arrangement applied to Margaret Douglas, Countess of Lennox, in 1565–6.[232] That this was considered a privilege is indicated both by the sex and status of the previous examples, and by the Lieutenant's instructions on the arrival of the Bishop of Lincoln in 1559: not only was he to treat him well, but as the Bishop was ill, he was 'wylled to have the rather regarde unto him and to spare him some of his owne lodging and stuff for the night'.[233]

The Haiward and Gascoyne survey clearly shows the Lieutenant's garden to the immediate north-west of his lodgings; this was directly accessible from the Lieutenant's house by stone steps.[234] In 1572 the garden was described as 'fensed but w$^{th}$ Lathes and the doore Locked in the nyght'.[235] It seems as though this wooden fence was only on the east side, the garden being protected by a brick wall on the north and west; it was not until 1605 that the eastern wall was rebuilt in brick at which time the others were heightened.[236] The 1597 survey simply shows a handful of trees but the garden was more than this: when in 1572 the alarm was raised at the sight of a man in the garden, it turned out to be the Lieutenant's undercook who had loosened the lathes 'to goo in to feche herbes',[237] while a hen-house was also within its walls.[238] In 1597 'postes and rayles' were set up in the Lieutenant's garden, suggesting that it was, in part at least, a formal Elizabethan garden.[239] Though the garden was technically the Lieutenant's, he seems often to have shared it with others as, for example, in 1533 when one Mr Foster had a chamber in the garden.[240] In the early years of the seventeenth century Sir Walter Ralegh's still house was in this garden and the door of his lodging in the Bloody Tower was described as 'always open all day to the garden'.[241]

## THE ORDNANCE STOREHOUSES

The great mass of gabled buildings which occupy the whole of the north end of the Inner Ward are not given a name on the 1597 survey. This is probably because they belonged to the Ordnance and Armoury offices, which were outside the jurisdiction of the Lieutenant of the Tower for whom the survey was made.

The Ordnance Office had been assigned buildings in the precincts of the Tower since the mid-fifteenth century.[242] By 1501 a house of ordnance stood within the Inner Ward and it was from here that Henry VII watched a tournament in that year.[243] In 1514 a new ordnance house was built to house the King's artillery, bows and arrows;[244] this was apparently in much the same location as that shown on the 1597 survey, being described at the time as 'upon the green within the Tower'.[245] However, the building was not to last long: by the autumn of 1533 it was already thought 'lykly to falle downe' and carpenters had to be employed to shore it up.[246] Despite this work the ordnance house was still considered to be in a dangerous state by an official report of February 1536.[247] Further repair work, particularly to the roof, was carried out in 1537;[248] but this was evidently not enough to stop plans for its demolition.

The building shown on the Haiward and Gascoyne survey was that built in 1545–7, apparently replacing its collapsing predecessor of 1514.[249] The new building was to be 'one house Wherin all the kinges maiesties Store and provicon of Artillerie Ordinnce and other Municons maye be kepte and garded and bestowed', though the account also refers to 'Rackes Wheron the kinges maiesties riche weapons and Artillerye were hanged and kept', indicating the Armoury Office used the building as well.[250] The building cost nearly £3,000, and the 1597 survey shows just how substantial the structure was.[251] Despite this huge expenditure, the building — like its predecessor — was found to be ill-equipped for its function: some of its floors were unable to support the weight placed on them and the main floor joists of the 'greate loft' were soon breaking.[252] Despite this, the building served as the principal ordnance storehouse until the end of the seventeenth century.[253] Indeed, it was sometimes even put to other uses, as is shown by the order to the Lieutenant of the Tower of 1552 'to remove Doctour Tunstall, late Bishop of Duresme from his lodging in thordinaunce Howse to summe other mete place, for that the sayd Ordinannce Howse must presently be occupyed otherwyse by the Officers of the same'.[254]

By 1641 the Ordnance Office's administrative rooms were located at the far west end of the great range of Ordnance buildings of 1545–7, and there is nothing to indicate they were elsewhere in the sixteenth century.[255]

## CHAPEL OF ST PETER AD VINCULA

The Chapel of St Peter ad Vincula, though unlabelled, is clearly shown to the north-west of the White Tower on the 1597 survey. The building as recorded on the survey and as survives today was built in Henry VIII's reign, although it was significantly restored in the nineteenth century at which time the windows were re-fashioned, the bell tower re-faced and the porch on the south front demolished.

The date of the construction of the first church or chapel on roughly the present site is unknown, though it may have been as early as the ninth century;[256] a church of this name was certainly in existence here by 1240 when Henry III ordered it be roofed. This building was demolished by Edward I and a new chapel constructed in its place in 1286–7.[257] In the first year of the sixteenth century the chapel was provided with seats and stalls for the use of the Knights of the Garter on the feast of St George.[258] Edward I's chapel stood until 1512, when it was destroyed by fire.[259] The construction of the new (existing) chapel seems to have begun in early 1519, and been completed in 1520.[260] As the building was only a decade or so old it was not mentioned in the great works estimate of 1532. The only attention it received in James Nedeham's building programme of the 1530s was new ironwork for the altar and minor repairs to the roof leads.[261]

As the royal family very seldom stayed at the Tower of London during the sixteenth century, the opportunities for it to function as a place of royal devotion were few. As well as being used by the Knights of the Garter in Henry VII's reign, the chapel was apparently used in the ceremonies of the creation of Knights of the Bath. In 1559, for example, the knights processed out of the White Tower to the chapel to hear mass.[262] In reality, however, St Peter ad Vincula was more the parish church of the Tower than the sovereign's chapel. The increase in the number of people living in the Liberties of the Tower in the course of Elizabeth I's reign caused Sir John Peyton to complain in 1597 that 'ther is not w$^{th}$in the Tower anie place sufficient for their burialls'.[263] The register of the chapel survives and gives incidental information about many of those buried in the chapel, showing them to have been both officers of the Tower and members of their families, and prisoners who had died during their term of imprisonment.[264]

In the reign of Edward VI the chapel's exemption from episcopal authority had been abolished and the Bishop of London's jurisdiction extended over it.[265] The chaplain of this modest chapel administered to a substantial parish: in 1596 it was reported of the Tower that 'the comunycantes there are said to be the nombre of 300'.[266] As well as the officers and staff of the Tower, some prisoners were allowed to attend divine service — a privilege which was keenly sought by many detainees.[267] One Catholic writer, however, tells of being 'dragged ... by military force to church', the Lieutenant boasting 'that there was no one in his fortress who did not go willingly to the Protestant church'.[268] The same writer describes a formal public debate between Edmund Campion and Protestant apologists 'in the public chapel of the fortress' suggesting that it was also used on occasion as a general room of assembly.[269]

## *X: Cole Harberte* — COLDHARBOUR GATE

The great gatehouse which gave access to the Inmost Ward of the Tower, known as Coldharbour, was probably built by Henry III. Today only its foundations remain, to the west of the White Tower, the building having been demolished in 1675–6.[270]

The great estimate of 1532 indicates that the intention was to rebuild the Coldharbour Gate: 'The tower callede Coldharber the same tow$^{r}$ the moste p[ar]te of it to be taken downe'. The stairs were to be mended and the stonework substantially replaced.[271] However, there is no mention of repairs to the gatehouse of any sort in the following decade, let alone a re-building.

As the 1597 survey shows, the Coldharbour Gate was still the principal entrance to the Inmost Ward in the sixteenth century and, as had presumably always been the case, a watch-house or porter's lodge operated either within, or very near, the gatehouse.[272] By the early sixteenth century the great cylindrical towers were also frequently used to house prisoners. It was from 'the prison of Colherberd' that Alice Tankerfelde made her escape in early 1534, shaking the inner door open after the bolt had fallen out, and opening the outer with a key procured from a servant of the Lieutenant.[273] Two of the sons of John Dudley, Duke of Northumberland, Ambrose and Henry, were probably housed in the Coldharbour Gate and in September 1553 were granted the 'liberty of the leades over Cole Harbert'.[274] The following year the gatehouse was apparently used to lodge some of Princess Elizabeth's attendants: Sir Henry Bedingfield enquired of the Council how he was to treat Elizabeth's servants 'lieng aboute the gate called colde harburgh'.[275]

By the late sixteenth century it seems that one of the drums of the gatehouse was known as 'Nun's Bower' and the other simply as 'Coldhabour'.[276] Both were repaired in 1590–1 when the lead roofs were replaced, the floors provided with new joists and the windows, jambs and doors mended.[277]

### *W: Cæsars or White Tower* — WHITE TOWER

The great keep of the fortress was built in the latter decades of the eleventh century, work beginning in the mid to late 1070s and finishing by 1100. Though the external walls themselves probably stood to their existing height from the beginning, it seems that until the end of the fifteenth century the White Tower contained only three storeys internally. The roof of the building was raised to its present level in about 1490, creating a full second floor for the first time.[278] The roof is incorrectly shown on the Haiward and Gascoyne plan to rise to one central ridge, perhaps reflecting the fact that, because of the 'bird's-eye' perspective of the plan, the surveyors had to record parts of the buildings which they had not themselves seen. As the White Tower was by far the tallest building in the fortress, its roof configuration was only visible from the top of the building itself. The survey is accurate, though, in showing a series of guns mounted on the roof; these had been a feature of the building since the reign of Henry VIII at the latest, and by the end of the century numbered about sixteen.[279]

Like much of the fortress, the White Tower was repaired in the 1530s: the first phase of work, of 1532–3, concentrated on the exterior of the building, perhaps to ensure that it formed a statuesque backdrop for Anne Boleyn's coronation procession. At this time the battlements and quoins were repaired,[280] while the roofs of the four turrets were replaced with cupolas — which remain today — and topped with gilded weather vanes.[281] Several years later the roof was substantially repaired.[282]

Although there is no evidence for royal residence of any sort in the White Tower during the Tudor period, the building continued to be used for one occasional ceremony during the century: the creation of Knights of the Bath on the eve of a coronation. Immediately before the coronation of Anne Boleyn eighteen baths were set up in the White Tower for the knights to bathe in, while rails were fixed from which hangings were suspended for the event.[283] Similar preparations no doubt preceded the creation of Knights of the Bath before the other coronations of the century.

Despite the occasional staging of this colourful medieval ritual, in the century preceding the execution of the Haiward and Gascoyne survey the White Tower was increasingly used for storage. Records of state had been kept in the White Tower in the fourteenth century, but were removed in 1360 when the captive King of France was to be lodged in the building. In 1568–70 works were carried out in the 'great Tower in the Tower of London' to prepare it for housing manuscripts again,[284] a function it retained until the mid-nineteenth century. The White Tower was also used to store armour: in the late 1560s 'twoe new Armouries' were fitted up in the White Tower,[285] while ten years later an estimate was submitted for 'makinge of romes within the great whytt Tower' also to house armour.[286] Some of the capacious rooms of the White Tower were commandeered too, by the Ordnance Office: by 1595 the keep was considered one of the traditional places for gunpowder storage,[287] while an inventory taken four years later records 2,299 barrels of 'Good and serviceable' powder in the White Tower.[288]

Though the White Tower was, by the end of the sixteenth century, essentially a great state storehouse, it was still occasionally used to house prisoners. The evidence suggests that the White Tower was only infrequently used for the detention of prisoners in this period and never for their long-term accommodation in the way the Bell, Beauchamp or Cradle towers functioned.[289] The building was also used, on occasion at least, for the torture of prisoners: John Gerard's account of his incarceration describes his torture in a large dark room with 'wooden post which held the roof of this huge underground chamber', all of which is consistent with the basement of the building before the insertion of the brick vaults in the eighteenth century.[290]

### *Y: Warderoap Tower* — WARDROBE TOWER

Like the Lanthorn and Bell towers, the Wardrobe Tower — today a ruin — stands on the line of the Roman wall of London. Remains of a Roman bastion incorporated into the existing fabric indicate that the medieval building was constructed on top of what remained of its Roman forebear. Though the date of the construction of the Wardrobe Tower, as shown on the Haiward and Gascoyne survey, is far from clear, it is usually ascribed to the second half of the twelfth century.[291]

The building later known as the Wardrobe Tower seems not to have had a fixed name in the sixteenth century, contemporary accounts describe it only in relation to other buildings: the 'rounde tower at the northwest end of the kyngs gardin', for example. The lack of a fixed name can make it tricky to identify in the accounts, but it seems that the Wardrobe Tower was the building for which carpenters provided a new roof in the autumn of 1532.[292] The tower which was rough-cast and had its battlements repaired by bricklayers at the same time also appears to have been the Wardrobe Tower.[293]

The earliest surviving written source to describe the tower immediately to the east of the keep as the 'Wardrobe Tower' (or rather, the 'Warderoap Tower') is, it seems, the 1597 survey. It is unclear whether the Wardrobe Tower itself was used as a repository for Wardrobe goods, or whether it was only known as such by association with the buildings which stood near it. The Tower of London had been an important repository for the goods managed by the Royal Wardrobe, and the various sub-sections into which it divided, throughout the Middle Ages. What this meant at about the time of the Haiward and Gascoyne survey is indicated by a description of the Master of the Wardrobe's responsibilities in a dictionary of 1613: 'he hath the charge and custodie of all former Kings and Queenes auncient Robes, remaining in the Tower of London, and all hangings of Arras, Tapestrie or the like, for his Majesties houses, with the bedding remaining in standing Wardrobes'.[294]

Immediately before the great programme of works of 1532 the Broad Arrow Tower was described as being 'at the ende of the wardrobe', indicating that the Wardrobe operated in the area around the Wardrobe Tower in the early sixteenth century.[295] It has been suggested that the eastern annexe of the White Tower, shown immediately to the west of the Wardrobe Tower on the 1597 survey, was also a Wardrobe repository, and though the evidence is inconclusive, it seems quite possible that this was the case.[296] The long building stretching east from the Wardrobe Tower to the Broad Arrow Tower shown on the 1597 survey was probably the 'new frame nowe made a warderobe for the kyng' of 1532, which measured 101 foot by 24 foot.[297] On the Haiward and Gascoyne survey only the south face of the building, with its three great chimney stacks, is visible. The principal entrance to the building was probably on the north side — it would have been very awkward to bring the often bulky charges of the Wardrobe in and out of the building through the royal garden. The Wardrobe was broken up into the department of 'robes' and that of 'beds', and though the two departments were technically separate, it seems that they both operated from the new long building of 1532.[298] The lead-roofed chamber which had belonged to 'my Lady the kynges grandmother', and which was converted for Wardrobe use in 1532, was clearly quite separate from the building adjoining the Wardrobe Tower and may well only have been used by the Wardrobe during the royal visit to the fortress in the spring of 1533.[299]

The Wardrobe at the Tower did not have a large staff and it seems its buildings were essentially repositories. As the majority of their charges — beds and robes — were textiles, the way they were stored was essential to their survival and, therefore, a regular supply of powder 'to make swete oure robes & apparell' and coals to air the collection was maintained, while cords were strung up 'to hange o^r^ apparrell on in ayringe of them'.[300]

### *Jewel House*

The Jewel House was the institution which, since the mid-fifteenth century, had managed the sovereign's collection of jewellery and precious metal goods. Highly valuable objects of this kind had actually been kept in the Tower of London since at least the fourteenth century, and by the sixteenth dedicated repositories, or jewel houses, were to be found within the fortress.

In the great estimate of 1532 one of the works which was described as 'not yet set in hand' was 'the offyce of the Juells hous to be newe made'.[301] This project eventually started early in 1535 and continued for just over a year. The detailed accounts of this work make it quite clear that there were two distinct Jewel House buildings in the Tower at this time: one which adjoined the White Tower, and one close to the White Tower but which adjoined 'the great buttery'.[302] The former is described in the accounts as having a lead roof and battlements, and was very probably that shown on the south front of the White Tower in 1597.[303] In January 1535 the jewel house adjoining the buttery was described as 'old', suggesting that the other — adjoining the White Tower — was the new jewel house in the Tower being built in 1508.[304]

In the course of 1535 the jewel house on the south face of the White Tower was given a new lead roof, while that which adjoined the buttery was rebuilt entirely.[305] The accounts reveal that the 'buttery' jewel house contained the administrative rooms of the institution: the building had an elaborate brick vaulted entrance from which stairs led up to the offices.[306] Over the vault was the closet, which was provided with 'a long settle with chests and seyllyng for backes to sytt upon and to leye books & other Records therin'; there was also a counting chamber[307] — 400 weights were provided 'for the waying of plates';[308] a waiting chamber which had the king and queen's arms in the windows,[309] and a privy.[310] As the building stood very close to both the White Tower and the other jewel house and had a vaulted entrance way, it is possible that it was the building shown running north-south at right angles to the jewel house on the south face of the White Tower on the 1597 survey.

In contrast to this, the 'White Tower' jewel house seems to have been simply a storehouse. It was provided with presses 'to sett plate and othere Juells there upon',[311] and chests with locks 'occupyed for plate & cases for the Juells'.[312] The windows were iron casements, also glazed with the king's badges in the glass.[313] This jewel house was reached by a vice and it is quite likely that it only partly occupied the building on the south face of the White Tower.[314] Before the works of 1535 began, an account refers to the two jewel houses by their different functions: 'the kinges stonding Jewel house' and the 'Jewelhouse were the kinges removing pate lyeth'.[315] The latter seems to have been the 'buttery' jewel house, which is described in the accounts for its rebuilding as 'a newe Juellhouse ... for the kyngs plate'.[316] The jewel house on the south front of the White Tower must, therefore, have been the standing jewel house, that is, home to a permanent collection of goods, in contrast to the removing jewel house, the contents of which would have been continually despatched out for use at other buildings. This identification of the jewel house on the south front of the White Tower as the standing jewel house would make sense of it simply being a storehouse, as the goods stored there would have been infrequently used.[317]

In addition to the repositories and administrative rooms contained within the Jewel House buildings, the lodging of the Keeper of the Jewel House was also to be found here, though it is unlikely he stayed here very often.[318] After the works of the 1530s the Jewel House buildings seem to have remained unaltered for the rest of the century; though various repairs are mentioned in the accounts, these amount to little more than mending the lead and tiles of the roofs.[319]

### *The Hall decayed*

The date of the construction of the first great hall in the Tower of London is obscure. A hall certainly existed in the early years of the reign of Henry III, and was substantially reconstructed during the 1220s and 1230s; how much, if any, of the old building was incorporated into Henry III's new hall is not certain. In the reign of Edward III the great hall received considerable attention: works included the repairing of the roof and the heightening of the north wall.[320]

In the sixteenth century, the hall was presumably used on the occasions when the royal family stayed at the Tower immediately preceding the coronations of Henry VII and Henry VIII. That the hall was in a poor state of repair in the early 1530s is indicated by the stated intention that 'The olde hall [is] to be taken downe and newe made';[321] as this was not included in the first sweep of works started in the summer of 1532, the existing structure was repaired rather than rebuilt in the months preceding the pre-coronation visit of Anne Boleyn and Henry VIII. All the works to the hall following the great estimate were carried out in the course of one month between 3 May and 1 June 1533. Bricklayers repaired the windows and doors, pargetted the porch, and rough-cast the exterior of the hall.[322] The roof leads were repaired[323] and the timber of the building — both internally and externally — was covered with yellow ochre.[324] Preparations were made within the building for its use: some of the windows were re-glazed,[325] the halpace, or dais, 'where the high Table stands' was paved with tiles,[326] trestle tables were built as was a chair of state for the King, which was to stand in the centre of the dais.[327] Joiners and carpenters were paid for the 'hasty fynyssyg' of the tables, forms and cupboards,[328] indicating work continued until the last moment — when brooms were supplied 'for the makyng clene of the hall'.[329]

In addition to these general repairs to the building, which are very much as would be expected, it appears from the works accounts that part of the west end of the hall was converted into a room for the Queen. Carpenters were paid for 'Tymbring & bording uppe of a p[ar]ticion in the west sid of the same hall for the quenes greatt chamb',[330] while masons placed new battlements on the west end of the hall,[331] and installed 'dyverse steppis of free ston goyng forthe of the said hall into the quenes chambr'.[332] It may have been in connection with this that the three doors at the end of the hall leading to the scullery, saucery and 'survaying place' were replaced.[333] The Haiward and Gascoyne survey and other sources indicate that the hall ran east-west just inside the inner curtain wall between the Wakefield and Lanthorn towers, with its principal door towards the west end. This would imply the west end of the hall was the service end, and the east the dais end, though the evidence is not as clear on this point as might be expected. Exactly what function a room for the Queen at the west end of the hall could have had is difficult to imagine.

In a sad irony, the hall so hastily prepared for the celebrations preceding the coronation of Anne Boleyn was next publicly used for her trial three years later. At this time 'a great scaffold' was made in the hall and 'benches and seates' for the lords, while the Duke of Norfolk sat beneath the cloth of estate as the King's representative.[334]

The haste with which the repairs to the hall were carried out in 1533 clearly prevented the building receiving the serious structural attention it required. If the hall was considered ready for rebuilding in 1532, it was in an even worse condition twenty-seven years later. A report on the state of the Tower of London submitted on 28 March 1559 put forward as its primary recommendation for 'reparacions' the hall, which 'is in very greate decaye so as it is lyke to fall if it bee not provided for in convenient tyme'.[335] There is no sign that it received any attention at all in the following seventeen years; and what small pieces of information there are about the hall in Elizabeth's reign suggest it was being gradually altered for other purposes. By the mid-1570s a brick wall had been built 'from the ground to the raysson [wall plate] by the hall pace Stayres at thend of thold hall',[336] while in 1590–1 the works accounts record 'quarteringe up y^e^ Northside of the hall where m^r^ Pigeon dweleth'.[337] The Haiward and Gascoyne plan shows only the north wall of the building standing, and — uniquely — makes a comment on the condition of the structure: 'decayed'. That this was indeed the level of dilapidation to which the hall had sunk by the end of the century is illustrated by the works to the building in preparation for the visit of James I: in 1603–4 both a new side wall and a roof were framed and set up, no attempt was made to provide a permanent roof covering, instead the fir rafters were simply 'to beare a Canvas coveringe' measuring 70 foot by 25 foot.[338]

### *The Queens Lodgings*

On the Whitehand and Society of Antiquaries' drawn copies of the Haiward and Gascoyne plan the series of buildings running north-south between the Wardrobe and Lanthorn towers is labelled 'The Queens Lodgings'. The description of these buildings as the 'queen's' in the reign of Elizabeth I would usually suggest that they were the apartments used by Elizabeth's father as sovereign, rather than consort's apartments. However, it seems in this instance that was not the case.

In the great estimate of 1532 the 'Rooffes and ffores of twoo chambres for the quene that ys to sey her prevy chambre and her dynyng chambre' were identified as requiring repair.[339] At this time Catherine of Aragon was still queen, and the Queen's chambers were probably constructed for one of her medieval predecessors. The intention to repair these rooms was apparently abandoned, in favour of re-building, in the summer of 1532; by September carpenters had 'taken downe the olde tymber of the quene dynyng chambre the frame thereof new made'.[340] The new great or dining chamber had a large bay window on the west side,[341] and a series of windows on the 'east syde next to the garden'.[342] At the north end, where steps led out of the building,[343] was a jakes or privy.[344] Overall the structure measured 59 foot by 26 foot[345] and was timber framed on brick foundations with brick gable ends.[346] The details of the Queen's great chamber strongly suggest it was the large north-south building shown next to the word 'Lodging' on the 1597 survey; although the accuracy of the measurements in this part of the survey is certainly questionable, according to Haiward and Gascoyne's own scale this structure has the same dimensions as that described in the accounts in 1532. Though one or two references are to be found in the 1530s to the Queen's 'old lodgings', it seems that the great, or dining, chamber was the only state room prepared for the Queen in 1532.

It has been suggested above that one of the two blocks to the north of the great chamber may have been part of the jewel house, and this is further supported by references in 1535 to 'the quenes utter chambr Joynyng to the new Juell house'.[347] If this was indeed the case, the eastern block was presumably the Queen's raying chamber, described in the accounts as 'next unto the said bakesyd of the said Juellhouse goyng into the leads ward nexto the greate gardeyn'.[348]

Thus it seems that while the King's apartments ran from the great hall to the Lanthorn Tower and the closet and gallery beyond, the Queen's apartments were entered from the north, and comprised the new great chamber of 1532, but then merged with the inner rooms of the King's apartments beyond.

In the course of Elizabeth I's reign, the hall, and perhaps others of the medieval state rooms used by Henry VIII, apparently fell out of use and instead the sequence of rooms used by Anne Boleyn were considered the monarch's lodgings. Certainly in 1603 the consort's great chamber of 1532 was considered the sovereign's great chamber: it was provided with elaborate new stairs, ornamented with finials,[349] as 'a new way for the Kinges Ma^tie^ to come to the privie lodginges neare to the Jewellhouse dore at the ende of the great chamber'.[350] It seems likely that this arrangement was informally established in Elizabeth's reign, when the absence of a consort made it unnecessary to provide two suites of rooms, and when it is known the hall was collapsing and the Ordnance Office using rooms within the royal lodgings to house stores.[351] This is also indicated by the Haiward and Gascoyne plan, which clearly shows as the 'Queens Lodgings' the range of buildings running north of the Lanthorn Tower.

### *The Queens Gallerie*

The gallery which is shown running between the Lanthorn and Salt towers was built along the line of the inner curtain wall in the spring and summer of 1506.[352] An innovative feature of a palace at the time it was erected, the first-floor gallery was one of the first built in a royal palace not as a covered access route but as a convenient room in which to perambulate and from which to view gardens.[353] Henry VII's gallery at the Tower ran between the great and privy gardens and, as was the case with other buildings of its sort in the early sixteenth century, a council chamber jutted off it.[354] The two small roofs of the council chamber can be seen to the north of the gallery on the 1597 survey.

As might be expected, the gallery was one of the buildings not mentioned in the works estimate of 1532, but which then featured prominently in the repairs subsequently carried out — once the prospect of a great royal visit was in sight. In the summer and autumn of 1532, therefore, the timber work of the windows was replaced,[355] and the windows themselves re-glazed,[356] the building was plastered and pargetted,[357] and the roof was re-tiled.[358] The royal visit of 1533 was only a short one and thereafter Henry VIII never stayed a night at the Tower; this did not, however, mean the royal rooms were unused. In December 1541 the Lieutenant of the Tower had written to the Council informing them that there was insufficient space in the fortress to lodge prisoners, 'unless the King and Queen's lodgings be taken', in which case the King's keys would be required to gain access to the rooms;[359] though the King had no memory of any keys, permission was immediately granted for the rooms to be used.[360] Therefore, when the twenty-three Scottish lords taken at the Battle of Solway Moss were brought *en masse* to the Tower in December 1542, various rooms in the King's apartments were prepared for their accommodation — among them the gallery in which several windows were repaired and reglazed 'Agenyst the comyng in of the prysoners of skottland'.[361]

In reality, occasions such as this were rare and the gallery seldom functioned as a prison lodging. However, privileged prisoners were sometimes given permission to walk in the gallery; for example in 1553 Viscount Hereford was to 'have the commoditie of the gardeyn and gallerye' because of 'his sicknes for want of ayer',[362] while the following year Princess Elizabeth's request 'to walke in the grette galorie' was referred by Sir Henry Bedingfield directly to the Privy Council.[363] The gallery continued, therefore, to function as a gallery: in the 1580s it was known as the prince's gallery, presumably in reference to its use by a visiting dignitary,[364] while in the mid-1590s the Lord Chamberlain ordered the cleaning of the gallery and several other rooms for the reception of the French envoy, the Duke of Bouillon.[365]

One of the reasons why the gallery was not commandeered for other uses in the sixteenth century may have been because it gave access to the council chamber overlooking the great garden. It seems that it was the council chamber adjoining the gallery, rather than that in the Lanthorn Tower, which was used by the Privy Council in the month following the death of Henry VIII[366] when they met frequently at the Tower.[367] Following the reading of Henry VIII's will and the appointment of Edward Seymour as Protector, it was from the council chamber that his executors despatched letters to the great foreign princes;[368] and it was here that they gathered again to make arrangements for the late King's funeral.[369] At such times when the Privy Council was meeting at the Tower the gallery could be an important place for private conference and discussion.[370]

### *R: The Lanthorne Tower*

The Lanthorn Tower was probably built by Henry III in the 1220s and it seems that while the Wakefield Tower, constructed at the same time, housed the sovereign's chamber, the Queen's chamber was within the Lanthorn Tower. Taller than the Wakefield, the Lanthorn Tower certainly contained three, and perhaps even four floors. In the reign of Edward II the King's chamber ceased to be in the Wakefield, and instead — certainly by 1340s — the Lanthorn Tower was the location of the King's inner rooms, an arrangement which was to continue for the next 300 years.[371]

Thus the Lanthorn Tower lay at the very heart of the Tudor royal lodgings: it contained both the King's bedchamber,[372] and a council chamber — apparently on the top floor, over the bedchamber.[373] After the construction of the new council chamber attached to the side of the long gallery in 1506, however, the council chamber in the Lanthorn Tower was probably little used. After 1506 access into the new royal gallery was, it seems, through the King's bedchamber — an arrangement which was to become common in early Tudor palaces.[374]

To the south of the Lanthorn Tower, the 1597 survey shows a small tower which straddled the Outer Ward between the Lanthorn and outer curtain wall. Described as 'the new towr at the weste ende of the kynges gallery' in 1532, this must be the new tower constructed by Henry VII in the autumn of 1501.[375] The building had two floors above the ground-level passage-way; the principal, upper floor was the innermost room of the King's apartments;[376] this functioned in the reign of Henry VII as the King's library, for which purpose the tower was presumably built.[377] In Henry VIII's reign the shelves of the library were taken down and the room was fitted up for devotion:[378] joiners provided an altar 'wrought rownde aboute the hedges wt antyk',[379] and 'a deske for his grace to knele upon'.[380] At the same time wainscot 'wrought wt Antyk' was also provided for the King's bedchamber.[381]

To the north-east and north-west of the Lanthorn Tower were the collection of rooms which comprised the King's apartments; none of these now survive. The earliest plans of the area post-date the demolition or drastic alteration of the principal rooms and most of the views of the Tower which show this area are confused.[382] Having said this, the exceptional detail given in the accounts for the preparation of these rooms for the visit of Henry VIII and Anne Boleyn do give some indication of their form and make a tentative reconstruction possible.[383]

The Henrician accounts reveal that two principal public chambers, other than the hall, were prepared for Henry VIII in 1532–3: these were the great watching chamber (or great chamber) and the presence or dining chamber.[384] The great watching chamber, always the first room entered after the hall in the sequence of Tudor state rooms, was in 1532 considered to require a new roof and floor.[385] In the course of the six months before the coronation in June 1533, carpenters carried out substantial repairs to the roof,[386] a clerestory was erected at the west end of the building and at the east end an area was partitioned off for the storage of fuel.[387] Plasterers were employed in 'yellow ockeryng' the timber work of the door and the stairs leading up to it, as they had done in the great hall.[388] The great watching chamber, then, was a structure which ran east-west, the principal floor of which was reached by an external staircase.[389] A list of necessary repairs of 1559 called for 'a fayre conveyance out to the said hall into the great chamber', indicating that it was necessary to pass outdoors from the great hall to enter the great watching chamber.[390]

The second state room after the great hall in the sequence was the presence or dining chamber. In preparation for Henry and Anne's visit bricklayers repaired the battlements and 'alle the wyndowes' along the east side of the chamber with brick and ragstone,[391] while freemasons re-made three windows 'from the transam upward'.[392] Within the room the old rotten ceiling was taken down and replaced in part with one removed from 'my Lady the kynges grandmother chambre',[393] while joiners installed new wainscoting and a mantelpiece 'wrought wt Antyk'.[394] Therefore, this was a chamber which ran north-south, and which had a number of windows on the eastern side; a reference to the 'garden sydde' of the chamber indicates that the windows looked on to the gardens.[395]

Taking this information about the King's apartments together with the ground- and first-floor surveys of the area around the Lanthorn Tower of 1731, some conclusions can be drawn.[396] First it seems likely that the presence/dining chamber was the building of which substantial sections still existed in the eighteenth century, which ran north from the junction between the Lanthorn Tower and the gallery. The first floor plan of 1731 indicates that this room had a series of windows along the eastern side, which would certainly have given a prospect of the great garden in the sixteenth century. It is further suggested that the building shown to the north of this, running east-west, on the 1731 plans had at its core an earlier building — parts of the thicker south, east and west walls of which can be seen embedded in the eighteenth-century building — and that this was the great watching chamber repaired for Henry VIII.[397] Therefore, it is suggested, the great watching chamber and presence chambers formed the north and east sides of a small courtyard, enclosed on the west side by the great hall and on the south by the chambers between the Lanthorn Tower and great hall. This courtyard was perhaps the 'kynges watchyng chamber warde' for which an entrance door was provided in 1532.[398]

In addition to the two large rooms slightly to the north-east of the Lanthorn Tower discussed above, the eighteenth-century plans show two slightly smaller buildings to the north-west of the Lanthorn Tower.[399] These, through some of which visitors would have passed to reach the King's bedchamber, gallery and closet from the larger outer chambers, probably housed the King's withdrawing chamber, and perhaps the King's grandmother's chamber and the King's raying chamber, though information about the form of these rooms is insufficient to say any more than this.

The 1597 survey is one of the very few images of this part of the fortress before its reconstruction in the seventeenth century. As has been mentioned above, Anne Boleyn's great chamber can be identified with the large north-south building standing alone next to the word 'lodging' on the Whitehand plan; the King's great (watching) chamber is perhaps the building which cuts across the south end of the Queen's great chamber, and the King's presence/dining chamber is probably the range which runs south from it along the same line as the Queen's great chamber, to meet the Lanthorn Tower at the point where it abuts the gallery. What does not tally is the depiction of two further north-south chambers to the north of the Lanthorn Tower on the Haiward and Gascoyne plan: these do not correspond with the two east-west buildings shown on the 1731 surveys, or with the Henrician documentary evidence. It can only be suggested that these, like the roof of the White Tower, were among those parts of the castle which the surveyors were unable to view, and the form of which they were, therefore, forced to guess.

During the short periods of royal residence at the Tower after the coronation of Anne Boleyn, the King's apartments were, of course, occupied: Edward VI received the Lord Mayor and aldermen of London under the cloth of estate in the presence chamber days after the announcement of his father's death,[400] while on the eve of Mary I's coronation the Knights of the Bath presented themselves here to be dubbed.[401] As these visits were infrequent the rooms of the royal apartments were to some extent put to other uses.[402] In the 1560s some of the sovereign's chambers were being used to store ordnance,[403] while once or twice during the century prisoners of the highest status were housed here. Four chambers in the royal lodgings were allocated to Princess Elizabeth when she was detained at the Tower in 1554, in addition to which she was given permission to walk in the great chamber 'nexte to hir owen chambers when so ever she comanndeth'.[404] The King's apartments were prepared to house the Scottish lords taken prisoner at Solway Moss: the King's great chamber, dining chamber, bedchamber and closet all being re-glazed for the occasion.[405] These must, however, be seen as exceptional uses of the rooms, and it is not until the reign of James I that the sovereign's apartments were used as prisoners' lodgings for any length of time; by the 1640s, though the Lanthorn Tower was still considered 'Part of y$^{e}$ Kings lodgings', the ground floor was described as 'a prison$^{rs}$ lodgeing'.[406]

### *The Pryvy garden*

In the reign of Henry VIII there were two royal gardens in the Tower of London separated from one another by the gallery running between the Lanthorn and Salt towers.[407] The larger garden to the north was known as the King's or great garden, that to the south as the Queen's or privy garden. The latter was a private enclosed area, separated from the 'laundress's' garden (perhaps some part of the Outer Ward to the west of the Lanthorn Tower) by a lockable door,[408] and from the great garden to the north by a gate 8 foot by 11 foot underneath the gallery.[409] Probably leading off this passageway between the gardens was 'the lytell chamber under the galery goyng into the quenes garden' to which various improvements were made in the 1530s[410] — including the provision of two new bay windows, a chimney and a jakes (a privy).[411] These details, and the location of this chamber, suggest it may have been a modest banqueting house of some sort.

The gardens could be reached from the royal lodgings in the Lanthorn Tower either by a door on the ground floor of the tower, which led straight into the privy garden (visible only on the Whitehand copy of Haiward and Gascoyne's plan), or from an upper level by an external staircase erected in the first years of the sixteenth century.[412] In the summer of 1532 timber and stone 'bridges' were constructed in both the royal gardens; the precise location and form of these bridges is unclear, though the description of one as adorned with six vanes,[413] indicates they were ornamental as well as functional.[414] The bridge in the King's garden was described as 'the new brydge over the brycke';[415] taken together with a reference to the 'Bryck walles in y$^{e}$ kinges gardens being very lowe' of 1606, this implies that the gardens in the Tower were divided up by low brick walls on which decorative posts and rails might be placed, as was frequently the case in Tudor royal gardens.[416]

Certainly from the mid-sixteenth century, and probably long before, access to the royal gardens at the Tower was a privilege allowed to a few chosen prisoners. Poor health, or particularly high status, could gain a prisoner this liberty: in June 1552, for example, the Privy Council gave permission for the Earl of Arundel to 'walke abrode in to the garden within the Tower at the discrecion of the Lieutenaunt of the Tower'.[417] In Mary I's reign Thomas Cranmer, Lady Jane Grey and Princess Elizabeth were all allowed to 'walke in the quenes garden',[418] the Privy Council having been told 'that diverse of them be and have byn evill at ease in their bodyes for want of ayre'.[419]

If the royal gardens at the Tower had been formal, ornamental affairs in the reign of Henry VIII, they did not long remain so. By the early 1570s the stairs were rotten, the great garden was 'noysomly kept w$^{th}$ weedes', indeed there were 'weedes layde at every Arch of the sayd Garden', the gate into the laundress's garden was missing while others had fallen down.[420] The 'Agas' plan of London of the mid-sixteenth century (Fig. 7) shows trees sprouting freely in this corner of the Tower, as does the 1618 Visscher panorama of London.[421] By the 1590s the Well and Cradle towers were being used to house prisoners and a little house for the watch was erected in the gardens.[422] The 1597 survey simply shows the royal gardens in the Tower as enclosed areas of ground with no indication of any vegetation at all; if this is not a reliable illustration of their appearance at this time, it does indicate how little importance was attached to them as royal gardens by the end of Elizabeth's reign.[423]

### *The Wharfe*

The great wharf at the Tower of London was built in stages during the fourteenth century. A timber structure stretched from Petty Wales (on the river just to the west of the Tower) to St Thomas's Tower by the end of the 1330s, this was replaced in stone in the 1360s, and extended to St Katharine's in the 1390s.[424]

The primary purpose of the wharf was as a place for unloading goods and the 1597 survey shows on the western half of the wharf two of the great cranes used for lifting goods to and from boats.[425] The Tower wharf was supposed to be used only for loading and unloading royal cargo, of which there must have been great quantities given that the Tower was the headquarters of military supply in England.[426] Buildings had stood on the eastern end of the wharf since at least the middle of the fifteenth century, at which time they were granted to the Master of the Ordnance as a place to store his charges.[427] By the reign of Henry VIII, though, 'all the buildings &c, on the wharf' belonged to the Master of the Armoury and so they remained throughout the century.[428] By the mid-sixteenth century the division of the wharf was formally recognized: the western end was 'to take all the ships ordnance, cables, anchors, armours and other sea munitions', while the east end was to 'be employed for bowyers, smiths fletchers carpenters and other crafts needed for the Tower'.[429]

By the end of Henry VIII's reign the wharf was in a bad state; although Sir Anthony Knevett was paid £48 2*s.* 3*d.* for repairs in 1546,[430] the verdict on the wharf in 1559 was that it 'is in great decaye, such as if it been not in convenient tyme loked unto, it wilbe a marvelous greate chardge to repayre it'.[431] Nothing more than piecemeal works ensued[432] until 1573–4 when the Master Mason of the Office of Works, Edward Yonge, carried out £156 6*s.* 4*d.* of repairs to the wharf.[433] This consisted of works to the sluice by the Byward Tower, 'takinge downe of a pece of olde wharfe', hewing and laying 3,500 foot of ashlar and 'fillinge of the walles with chalke and hardestone all a longe the wharfe behinde his newe worke'. This was finished off by further in-filling with oyster shells and 'good Rubbishe' and covering-over with gravel.[434] The following year the Sergeant Painter was at work painting the 'greate postes railes and ballesters' on either side of the royal landing stairs opposite the Byward gate; the posts were topped with vanes featuring the royal arms lavishly painted in gold.[435]

Despite these substantial works of the 1570s, even more extensive repairs were carried out right through the 1590s.[436] These began with a variety of repairs to the wharf and landing stairs, 'where the water had eaten and p[er]ished y$^{e}$ same'.[437] Houses on the wharf were pulled down, the Byward postern drawbridge rebuilt and the sluice 'which was fallen downe into the moate' repaired.[438] It was also at this time that the great brick wall, which can be seen stretching much of the length of the wharf on the 1597 survey, was erected. It appears that the first section, from the Bulwark to the south end of the Byward postern drawbridge, was erected in 1592–4,[439] and that the second, on to the eastern end of the wharf, was erected in 1594–5. The estimate for the second section describes the wall as measuring 822 feet and standing 9 feet tall, and stretching from 'a peece of a new wall lately made neere to the ward house' to the 'Crosse wall neere the Iron gate neere S$^{t}$ katherins',[440] it was duly constructed and fitted with three stone doorways.[441]

It seems probable that the great wall was built to improve the security of the wharf, which was a recurrent concern in the sixteenth century. The moat was at its narrowest on the south side, allowing prisoners to communicate with people passing on the wharf, and even — on occasion — to cross the moat to the wharf and a boat to freedom.[442] In 1572 a report on the state of the Tower of London recommended 'That the Tower wharffe be shutt up, so as none resorte thiter but suche as ought to attend for service there or have just cause to come into the Tower'.[443] Orders against 'comon accesse' to the wharf were issued again in 1582 and concern was expressed that only Englishmen should be allowed to dwell there.[444] The construction of a 9 foot wall would have made it much harder to reach the Thames from the southern moat — in fact John Gerard's escape nearly foundered on this very difficulty of overcoming the high wall built only two years earlier.[445]

In 1595–7 the wharf itself was strengthened with new campsheds and both the common stairs (at the far west end of the wharf), and the privy stairs (presumably the royal landing stairs) were mended with hard stone, the latter being given new posts and rails.[446] A secondary function of the Tower wharf was as the landing place for official visitors; foreign dignitaries and ambassadors making their state entries to the country would disembark their boats at the wharf, where they would enter coaches to make the rest of the journey to court.[447] The royal stairs were frequently used for this purpose, and some, if not all of the works in the mid-1590s, were intended to make the wharf a suitably handsome structure for the ceremonial reception of foreign ambassadors.[448]

In 1598–9 nearly £500 was spent on 'repayringe of the Quenes Ma^ts^ privie stayres and wharf', and works continued after the Haiward and Gascoyne survey was taken, throughout the last years of Elizabeth's reign. In February 1601 the Office of Works reported that the £3,168 usually reserved for the Queen's use had in the past three years been spent on the new banqueting house at Whitehall, and 'repairing the Tower wharf'.[449]

## NOTES

[1] C. L. Kingsford (ed.), *A Survey of London by John Stow Reprinted from the Text of 1603*, 2 vols. (Oxford, 1908), I, p. 48. In John Skelton's verses on the death of Edward IV, the King's spirit numbered among his achievements: 'I made the Tower strong', quoted in S. Thurley, *The Royal Palaces of Tudor England* (New Haven and London, 1993), p. 18. For a detailed discussion of the history of the Bulwark see Geoffrey Parnell's contributions to M. Hutchinson, 'Edward IV's Bulwark: excavations at Tower Hill, London, 1985', *Transactions of the London and Middlesex Archaeological Society* 47 (1996), pp. 103–44.
[2] Quoted in H. Colvin (ed.), *The History of the King's Works*, 6 vols. (London 1962–82), II, p. 729.
[3] *Calendar of the Close Rolls preserved in the Public Record Office: Edward IV, Edward V, and Richard III AD 1476–1485* (London, 1954), p. 379.
[4] W. D. Hamilton (ed.), *A Chronicle of England during the Reigns of the Tudors from AD 1458 to 1559 by Charles Wriothesley, Windsor Herald*, Camden Society, NS 11 and 20, 2 vols. (London, 1875–77), I, p. 179. The remains of the wall which surrounded the Bulwark are represented in a dark red in Johann Spilberg II's view of the Tower of *c.* 1691.
[5] *The Chronicle of Queen Jane and Two Years of Queen Mary*, ed. J. G. Nichols, Camden Society, 48 (London, 1850), p. 55; Hamilton (ed.), *A Chronicle of England*, I, p. 179; BL, Add. MS 14044, f. 15v.
[6] See Hutchinson, 'Edward VI's Bulwark', pp. 109, 113. In 1514 labourers were employed 'drawing culverings into the Bulwark'; J. S. Brewer *et al.* (eds.), *Letters and Papers, Foreign and Domestic, of the Reign of Henry VIII, 1509–47* (hereafter *L&P*) 23 vols. (London, 1862–1932), 1513–14, p. 1481.
[7] These gates, provided with locks and bolts, were repaired in 1536, 1590–1 and again in 1601–2, Bod. Lib., Rawl. MS D 780, f. 247r; PRO, E351/3225; 3237.
[8] *Calendar of State Papers Domestic Series of the reign of Mary I 1553–1558* (hereafter *CSPD Mary*), ed. C. S. Knighton (London, 1998), p. 121; BL, Add. MS 14044, f. 40v.
[9] Bod. Lib., MS Eng Hist e 195, f. 3r. In 1606 it was complained that the Bulwark '... is quite within a few years made of no use by buildings from one end to the other', quoted in Hutchinson, 'Edward IV's Bulwark', p. 114.
[10] G. Parnell, *The Tower of London* (London, 1993), pp. 76–7.
[11] Colvin (ed.), *The History of the King's Works*, II, pp. 720–1; G. Parnell, *The Royal Menagerie at the Tower of London*, Royal Armouries exhibition catalogue 1999, pp. 6–7.
[12] PRO, E101/474/18. This extraordinary estimate for works to the Tower is actually undated, but the strong likelihood is that it was made in 1532, and so for ease of reference it is assumed throughout this gazetteer to be of this date.
[13] BL, Egerton MS 2358, f. 16r.
[14] Bod. Lib., Rawl. MS D 775, f. 202r.
[15] *L&P*, January-June 1536, p. 111.
[16] PRO, E351/3216. It may be that this was not entirely successful, as a new bridge at the gate by the lions was again being constructed in 1596–7, PRO, E351/3231.
[17] The lion keeper's house was certainly in this location in the following century, when it was rebuilt: Parnell, *The Royal Menagerie*, p. 9.
[18] PRO, E351/3238.
[19] *L&P*, 1515–16, pp. 116–17; January-July 1544, p. 189; C. Williams, *Thomas Platter's Travels in England, 1599* (London, 1937), p. 163.
[20] *John Gerard: the Autobiography of an Elizabethan*, translated by Philip Caraman (London, 1951), pp. 122–3.
[21] Colvin (ed.), *The History of the King's Works*, II, p. 721.
[22] *L&P*, 1509–13, p. 126; 1517–18, p. 1106; BL, Harl. MS 1326, f. 125r. J. Craig, *The Mint: a History of the London Mint from AD 287 to 1948* (Cambridge, 1953), p. 31.
[23] The extent to which the Haiward and Gascoyne plan fixed formally names for buildings which had hitherto been fluid should not be underestimated, in many cases the nomenclature on the plan is not to be found in any written sources prior to 1597, but has been frequently used since; for example: the Middle Tower, the Wardrobe Tower, the Salt Tower and the Flint Tower.
[24] PRO, SP12/3, 46.
[25] PRO, E351/3231.
[26] Colvin (ed.), *The History of the King's Works*, II, p. 716.
[27] Stow, *Survey of London*, I, p. 49.
[28] PRO, E101/474/18.
[29] PRO, E351/3231.
[30] BL, Add. MS 14044, f. 7v.
[31] Stow, *Survey of London*, I, p. 49; Hamilton (ed.), *A Chronicle of England*, II, p. 7; J. G. Nichols (ed.), *Chronicle of the Grey Friars of London*, Camden Society 53 (London, 1852), p. 57.
[32] BL, Harl. MS 1326, f. 125r.
[33] Bod. Lib., Rawl. MS D 778, ff. 51r, 52v. J. R. Dasent (ed.), *Acts of the Privy Council of England* (hereafter *APC*), 32 vols. (London, 1890–1907), IX, p. 163.
[34] PRO, SP11/6, f. 51r.
[35] PRO, E351/3231.
[36] See R. Allen Brown and P. Curnow, *Tower of London* (London, 1984), p. 39.
[37] E. Impey and G. Parnell, *The Tower of London* (London, 2000), p. 113.
[38] Bod. Lib., MS Eng Hist e 195, f. 5v.
[39] '... Then neare within this west gate opening to the south is a strong posterne, for passengers, by the wardhouse, over

a draw bridge, let down for that purpose'; Stow, *Survey of London*, I, p. 49.
[40] *The Chronicle of Queen Jane*, p. 70.
[41] PRO, E351/3231, and 3234.
[42] Parnell, *The Tower of London* (1993), pp. 37, 43.
[43] PRO, E101/474/18.
[44] Parnell, *The Tower of London* (1993), col. pl. 8, pp. 59–60; J. Charlton (ed.), *The Tower of London: its Buildings and Institutions* (London 1978), p. 117.
[45] PRO, SP12/3, 46.
[46] PRO, SP12/33, 64.
[47] Parnell, *The Tower of London* (1993), pp. 37–8, 43–5.
[48] 'The Martin Tower Over against the green Mount', BL, Harl. MS 1326, f. 125r.
[49] Compare Colvin (ed.), *The History of the King's Works*, II, p. 718 and Parnell, *The Tower of London* (1993), pp. 48–9.
[50] PRO, E101/474/18.
[51] BL, Harl. MS 1326, f. 125r.
[52] Colvin (ed.), *The History of the King's Works*, II, pp. 718–19, 724, 728; Parnell, *The Tower of London* (1993), pp. 48–9.
[53] The 1597 survey shows that access to the eastern drawbridge from the body of the fortress was not easy: the privy garden stood between the curtain walls to the west and a building with stepped gables spanned the outer ward to the north.
[54] PRO, E101/474/18.
[55] Bod. Lib., Rawl. MS D 778, f. 62r.
[56] *L&P*, January-June 1536, p. 111.
[57] Bod. Lib., Rawl. MS D 780, ff. 247r-251v.
[58] BL, Add. MS 14044, f. 41r.
[59] *APC*, IX, p. 163.
[60] PRO, E351/3227.
[61] PRO, E351/3228.
[62] Stow, *Survey of London*, I, p. 49.
[63] BL, Harl. MS 1326, f. 125r.
[64] Colvin (ed.), *The History of the King's Works*, II, p. 718.
[65] Allen Brown and Curnow, *Tower of London*, p. 84.
[66] The springing of the archway can still be seen, Allen Brown and Curnow, *Tower of London*, p. 84.
[67] PRO, E101/474/13, f. 17v. While the Whitehand copy of the 1597 survey shows a path running north from the Queen's Gallery across the great garden, no such path is indicated in the 'pryvy garden' (see the entry for the privy garden, below).
[68] PRO, E101/474/18.
[69] PRO, E101/474/13, f. 2v.
[70] *Royal Commission on Historic Monuments (England): An Inventory of the Historical Monuments in London,* 5 vols. (London, 1924–30), V, p. 79.
[71] PRO, E351/3228. The Well Tower might even be the 'prison in the previe garden' mentioned in 1600–1, PRO, E351/3236.
[72] BL, Harl. MS 1326, f. 125r.
[73] Colvin (ed.), *The History of the King's Works*, II, pp. 725–6.
[74] *John Gerard: the Autobiography of an Elizabethan*, pp. 128–35; *Historical Manuscripts Commission: Calendar of the Manuscripts of the Marquess of Salisbury at Hatfield House*, 24 vols. (London, 1883–1976), VII, pp. 417–18.
[75] It was the unexpected barring of the door on to the leads by Arden's warder which prevented Gerard and Arden's first escape attempt from going as planned.
[76] Stow, *Survey of London*, I, p. 49.
[77] Colvin (ed.), *The History of the King's Works*, II, pp. 718–20; S. Thurley, 'Royal lodgings at the Tower of London 1216–1327' *Architectural History* 38 (1995), pp. 47–51, 54.
[78] *L&P*, 1532, p. 491.
[79] PRO, E101/474/12, f. 4r.
[80] Ibid., f. 3r.
[81] PRO, E101/474/12, f. 4v; E101/474/13, f. 9r.
[82] PRO, E101/474/13, f. 1r.
[83] Ibid., f. 8r.
[84] PRO, SP12/33, 64.
[85] Bod. Lib., Rawl. MS D 775, ff. 202r, 206r, 211v.
[86] Bod. Lib., Rawl. MS D 775, f. 206r.
[87] *The Chronicle of Queen Jane*, pp. 67, 73–4. Regardless of the charge against them, prisoners of higher status were invariably allocated the more comfortable lodgings; as Courtenay was the Queen's cousin it is not surprising that he should have been given some of the most pleasant rooms in the fortress.
[88] The building was certainly somewhat neglected during the reign: in about 1570 it was reported that the watergate was 'very fillthy and fowle' while the stairs of the basin were 'sore decayed', BL, Add. MS 14044, f. 41v. This was no doubt remedied to some degree by the works of the early 1570s which included the provision of new gates and repairs to the arch, PRO, E351/3206; 3209.
[89] BL, Harl. MS 1326, f. 125r.
[90] BL, Add. MS 14044, f. 36r.
[91] *The Chronicle of Queen Jane*, p. 70; though — interestingly — this story was already being told during her lifetime: 'we came to a grating through which criminals are lead, the queen was also brought this way.' Williams, *Thomas Platter's Travels in England 1599*, p. 163.
[92] Colvin (ed.), *The History of the King's Works*, II, p. 722; Parnell, *The Tower of London* (1993), pp. 43–4; Craig, *The Mint*, pp. 57–8.
[93] *L&P*, 1513–14, pp. 1511, 1349, 1392, 1416, 3410.
[94] *L&P*, 1526–8, p. 2236.
[95] *L&P*, 1526–7, p. 2237.
[96] Ibid.
[97] The Outer Ward does seems to have been considered the domain of the Mint, in 1559 — for example — an area of the outer curtain wall which was in decay was described as 'on the farther syde of the mynt', PRO, SP12/3, 46.
[98] PRO, E351/3200.
[99] Craig, *The Mint*, p. 120; H. Symonds, 'The Mint of Queen Elizabeth and those who worked there', *The Numismatic Chronicle,* 4th series, XVI (1916), p. 65; PRO, E351/3200.
[100] PRO, E351/3200.
[101] It has been suggested (Colvin (ed.), *The History of the King's Works*, III, p. 270) that the new upper mint of 1560–1 was next to the Salt Tower in the Outer Ward because of a reference of 1581–2 to 'the Minte houses by the Salte Towre'; however, there were clearly many Mint buildings within the Tower by this time and the buildings by the Salt Tower need not have been the same as the new building of 1560–1.
[102] PRO, E351/3237. The meaning of these terms (if any) in the context of the topography of the Tower is ambiguous.
[103] PRO, E351/3203.
[104] PRO, E351/3219; some years before it had been reported that 'much of the lead [was] stollen away from over the mynt', BL, Add. MS 14044, f. 41r.

[105] PRO, SP12/33, 64, five platforms were to be provided 'upon the leads' at the Mint.
[106] This was apparently in the upper mint area of the Tower; Symonds, 'The Mint of Queen Elizabeth', p. 70. However it is possible that the 'mill' which gave the 'Mill Mint' its name was, instead, that which had been erected by one Mr Brocke in Queen Mary's reign; R. Lemon (ed.), *Calendar of State Papers, Domestic Series, of the reigns of Edward VI, Mary, Elizabeth 1547–1580* (London, 1856), p. 133.
[107] 'From there we went to the Mint, where on either side many persons were sitting and working continously.' Victor von Klarwill (ed.), *Queen Elizabeth and some Foreigners* (London, 1928), p. 318; W. B. Rye (ed.), *England as Seen by Foreigners* (London, 1865), p. 19.
[108] Symonds, 'The Mint of Queen Elizabeth', p. 67.
[109] BL, Lansdowne MS 14, f. 16r.
[110] PRO, E351/3216. Among these, as well as the workshops for producing the coins, were rooms for the moneyers themselves, including the coiners' kitchen and the coiners' hall; BL, Add. MS 14044, ff. 41r-v.
[111] Similar dotted lines also section-off the north-west and north-east corners of the moat, which on the plan are marked with crosses. These presumably denoted that someone other than the Lieutenant was responsible for, or had rights over, these sections of the moat.
[112] Colvin (ed.), *The History of the King's Works*, II, pp. 708–10.
[113] 'The wall from Seynt Thoms tower unto the foregate ov^r^ against bell tow^r^ ... clx ffoote', PRO, E101/474/18.
[114] 'the wall from the same garden tower [Bloody Tower] unto bell tow^r^ adjoynyg to m^r^ lieutenntes house', PRO, E101/474/18.
[115] Allen Brown and Curnow, *Tower of London,* pp. 44–5.
[116] PRO, E101/474/18.
[117] In 1641 the tower was described simply as 'Adjoining to ye L^ts^ house a prison lodgeing', BL, Harl. MS 1326, f. 125r.
[118] BL, Royal MS 17 D. XIV, f. 429v.
[119] See under the Lanthorn Tower below.
[120] 'the leivetannant ... came to him in his chamber in the Bell Tower, finding him yet a sleepe in his bedd; and waked him ... he tould him at last that he was come to signifie unto him, that the kings pleasure was he should suffer death that forenoone', Fr. Van Ortroy (ed.), *Vie du Bienheureux Martyr Jean Fisher Cardinal, Eveque de Rochester* (Brussels, 1893), p. 337.
[121] *The Chronicle of Queen Jane*, p. 67.
[122] *The Chronicle of Queen Jane*, p. 33. This was a liberty allowed to various prisoners, among them Sir John York, arrested for supporting Lady Jane Grey, in the month before his release. Ibid., p. 27.
[123] PRO, E351/3205; E351/3225. Wenceslaus Hollar's engraving of the execution of the Earl of Strafford in 1641 shows the bell house perched on the roof of the Bell Tower much as today.
[124] *John Gerard: the Autobiography of an Elizabethan*, p. 111.
[125] E. Impey, 'The western entrance to the Tower of London, 1240–41', *Transactions of the London and Middlesex Archaeological Society* 48 (1997), p. 72.
[126] *RCHME London,* V, pp. 84–6, records 126 separate inscriptions within the building, the vast majority of those with dates are of the mid- to late sixteenth century.
[127] *L&P*, January-July 1535, p. 397.
[128] Lady Jane Grey was kept in this area; from her lodging she 'loking throughe the windowe sawe the duke and the rest going to the churche', *The Chronicle of Queen Jane*, p. 19.
[129] *L&P*, January-May 1537, p. 255.
[130] *The Chronicle of Queen Jane*, p. 27.
[131] PRO, SP12/85, 6.
[132] Graffiti in his name on the second storey is dated 22 June 1587.
[133] PRO, E351/3229.
[134] PRO, E351/3226.
[135] PRO, E351/3238.
[136] BL, Harl. MS 1326, f. 125r. The works account for 1603–4 refer to 'taking upp. all the boordes of the ould flower in the second storie of Beuchamp. Tower where the Lord Cobham lyeth'; PRO, E351/3239.
[137] Colvin (ed.), *The History of the King's Works*, II, p. 711.
[138] Allen Brown and Curnow, *Tower of London*, p. 79.
[139] PRO, E101/474/18.
[140] PRO, E101/474/12, f. 4r.
[141] PRO, E101/474/12, f. 4v.
[142] PRO, E101/474/12, f. 5r; E101/474/13, f. 8r.
[143] PRO, E101/474/13, f. 5v.
[144] *The Chronicle of Queen Jane*, p. 55.
[145] J. Bayley, *The History and Antiquities of the Tower of London,* 2 vols. (London, 1825), I, p. 179.
[146] *The Chronicle of Queen Jane*, pp. 46–7. In the estimate for new gun platforms for the fortress dated 1564, the Devereux Tower was to be provided with a platform 33 foot by 25 foot, PRO, SP12/33, no. 64.
[147] Hollar's engraving of the execution of the Earl of Strafford and Johann Spilberg II's view of the Tower both show a squarish building immediately to the south of the Devereux Tower, apparently incorporating the curtain wall, the name and function of which is unknown.
[148] It certainly was in the early eighteenth century, when works were carried out in and about the building 'for Furbishers & Gunsmiths', quoted in Parnell, *The Tower of London* (1993), p. 95.
[149] Bayley, *The History and Antiquities of the Tower of London*, I, p. 180.
[150] Colvin (ed.), *The History of the King's Works*, II, pp. 711–12.
[151] In the first years of the sixteenth century 'Bower's Tower', perhaps this building, was given new doors 'for the better fortification' of it, and doors and a window strengthened with iron bars. BL, Egerton MS 2358, f. 15r.
[152] PRO, SP12/33, 64.
[153] BL, Harl. MS 1326, f. 125r.
[154] Bayley, *The History and Antiquities of the Tower of London*, I, p. 181.
[155] PRO, E101/474/18.
[156] 'for coveryng of the hedys of iiii Turretts the wyndelesses that is to sey in Bowyars [Flint] Tower and Burbegge [Bowyer] Tower next unto it ...', PRO, E101/474/13, f. 7v.
[157] PRO, SP12/33, 64. Like the Flint, the Bowyer was probably one of the 'london' towers mentioned in 1641.
[158] Bayley, *The History and Antiquities of the Tower of London*, I, p. 181.
[159] *L&P*, 1517–18, pp. 1458, 1460.
[160] PRO, E101/474/18.
[161] Bayley, *The History and Antiquities of the Tower of London*, I, p. 181.

[162] BL, Harl. MS, 1326, f. 125r.
[163] *APC*, III, p. 403.
[164] In the 1530s the Middle Tower was still being called the 'Martin', and the Martin Tower is not given a proper name. In fact the building, though called the 'Martin' on the Haiward and Gascoyne plan, has rarely been known as such over the past 500 years. In the mid-seventeenth century it was the Irish Tower, while from the 1670s to the 1840s — when it housed the regalia — it was known as the Jewel Tower.
[165] PRO, E101/474/18.
[166] BL, Harl. MS 1326, f. 125r.
[167] PRO, E351/3231.
[168] Impey and Parnell, *The Tower of London*, p. 80.
[169] PRO, E351/3229.
[170] PRO, E351/3232.
[171] PRO, E351/3235.
[172] PRO, E351/3235. The works estimate of 1532 had included costs for replacing the roofs of the two small turrets, but there is no sign this work followed, E101/474/18.
[173] PRO, E351/3236.
[174] PRO, Harl. MS 1326, f. 125r.
[175] PRO, SP12/3, 46. This was reiterated a decade or so later, when the Constable's lodging was again described as 'ready to fall' as it 'sincketh downe', BL, Add. MS 14044, f. 41v.
[176] PRO, E351/3236.
[177] On the survey of 1682 the three houses in this area were described as belonging to the Clerk of the Ordnance, the King's Storekeeper and the Surveyor of the Ordnance. As has been pointed out elsewhere (Charlton (ed.), *The Tower of London*, p. 75) several eighteenth-century plans of the Tower call a substantial building adjacent to the Lanthorn Tower the 'Constable's House', but there is nothing in the extensive details of works to this area of the fortress in the sixteenth century to suggest any room here was known by this name at that time.
[178] PRO, E351/3238.
[179] Allen Brown and Curnow, *Tower of London*, p. 75.
[180] PRO, E101/474/13, f. 7v.
[181] PRO, E101/474/13, f. 5r.
[182] 'Carpenters ... And more made ii turretts w^t^ a Roffe and Joystes to the same Tower one of the Turretts w^t^ an Awlter', PRO, E101/474/13, f. 1r. It is possible the altar was not a new addition at this date but mentioned only to indicate which tower was meant; however this seems unlikely — although these accounts are detailed they almost never refer to anything other than the work actually done.
[183] BL, Harl. MS 1326, f. 125r.
[184] PRO, E351/3232.
[185] PRO, E101/474/12, f. 4r; E101/474/13, f. 1r. These were replaced again sixty years later, when various general repairs were done to the Salt Tower, E351/3226.
[186] PRO, E101/474/12, f. 5r; E101/474 13, f. 7v.
[187] PRO, E101/474/12, f. 4v; E101/474/13, f. 5r.
[188] PRO, E101/474/13, f. 10v.
[189] PRO, E101/474/12, f. 5v.
[190] Colvin (ed.), *The History of the King's Works*, II, p. 725.
[191] 'Mending of y^e^ Tour called Salt Tour where m^r^ John Parot Laye', PRO, E351/3225.
[192] Thus the two prisoners being detained in the Salt Tower in 1572, 'Powell and Barthe', were doubtless kept one above the other on the first and second floors. PRO, SP12/85, 6.
[193] *John Gerard: the Autobiography of an Elizabethan*, pp. 104–6.
[194] BL, Harl. MS 1326, f. 125r.
[195] Thurley, 'Royal lodgings at The Tower of London 1216–1327', pp. 36–57.
[196] PRO, E101/474/18; *L&P*, 1509–13, p. 537; 1515–16, p. 520. Even in the late seventeenth century only the western end of this building was used by the record office, the eastern being by this time the lodging of the Treasurer of the Ordnance.
[197] PRO, E351/3214.
[198] See for example, *L&P*, 1534, p. 126, and *APC*, V, p. 296.
[199] For example, *L&P*, 1509–13, p. 537; BL, Harl. MS 1326, f. 125r.
[200] P. Curnow, 'The Bloody Tower', in Charlton (ed.), *The Tower of London*, pp. 55–61; Allen Brown and Curnow, *Tower of London*, pp. 49–53; Colvin (ed.), *The History of the King's Works*, II, pp. 711, 719, 726. As ever I am grateful to Jeremy Ashbee for sharing and discussing with me his work on the medieval royal apartments.
[201] Colvin (ed.), *The History of the King's Works*, I, p. 726 note 1.
[202] The Heath version of the plan shows this portcullis, but it is not shown on either the Whitehand or the Antiquaries' copies. It may be that this detail was added by Joseph Heath.
[203] PRO, E351/3203.
[204] 'Coming out of the Bloody Tower, so named because of King Richardus having there most miserably put to death his two young cousins who were placed under his guardianship, we came to Mint street ...', in 'Diary of the Journey of the Duke of Stettin-Pomerania 1602', *Transactions of the Royal Historical Society*, second series, VI (1892), p. 17.
[205] When William Rossey suggested to the Council in April 1556 that they pretend to have a good opinion of one Staunton, a prisoner in the Tower, by telling him that he was to be housed 'in some better lodging', the Bloody Tower was the building he recommended, *CSPD Mary*, p. 193.
[206] *L&P*, January-July 1535, pp. 397–8.
[207] *The Chronicle of Queen Jane*, p. 27.
[208] PRO, SP12/85, 6, dated 12 January 1571/2.
[209] PRO, E351/3241; this floor was later removed, and then reinstated in the 1970s.
[210] July 1540, payment to Walsingham of '100*l.* to be employed about the new building of his dwelling house and other necessaries', *L&P*, January-August 1540, p. 189.
[211] That the previous building was certainly in the same position is shown by the great works estimate of 1532 which gives details of 'the wall from the garden [Bloody] tower unto bell tow^r^ adjoynyng to m^r^ lietenntes house' PRO, E101/474/18.
[212] Parnell, *The Tower of London* (1993), p. 50; Allen Brown and Curnow, *Tower of London*, p. 70 and fig. 18. Although the medieval stonework embedded within the Tudor building is thought to be fourteenth century in date, it is not absolutely certain that this was the building provided for the Constable of the Tower in the 1360s.
[213] PRO, E101/474/18.
[214] Bod. Lib., Rawl. MS D 777, f. 119v.
[215] *L&P*, August-December 1539, pp. 110, 151, 176.
[216] Parnell, *The Tower of London* (1993), pp. 58–9.

[217] 'newe makinge of a foot pace in m^r^ Leiuetennes halle', PRO, E351/3228.
[218] PRO, E351/3238.
[219] The 'Agas' map of London (Fig. 7) also clearly shows a substantial window serving a double-height room in one of the gable bays facing south in this position. Interestingly the window remained after the hall was split into two, as Hollar's watercolour of the mid-seventeenth century (Fig. 9) shows.
[220] *John Gerard: the Autobiography of an Elizabethan*, p. 120.
[221] PRO, E351/3238.
[222] The private rooms would have included those used by the Lieutenant's family, see, e.g. PRO, E351/3219.
[223] PRO, E351/3228.
[224] PRO, E351/3225; E351/3228.
[225] PRO, E351/3229.
[226] PRO, E351/3232.
[227] *APC*, VII, p. 94.
[228] *APC*, VIII, p. 21.
[229] R. Lemon and M. A. Everett Green (ed.), *Calendar of State Papers Domestic in the Reign of Elizabeth* (hereafter *CSPD*), 5 vols (London, 1865–70) 1591–4, p. 24.
[230] PRO, E351/3237.
[231] *APC*, IV, p. 20.
[232] *RCHME London*, V, p. 95.
[233] *APC*, VII, p. 78.
[234] PRO, E351/3229.
[235] PRO, SP12/85, no. 6.
[236] *HMC Salisbury*, XVII, pp. 379, 388; BL, Add. MS 14044, f. 9r.
[237] PRO, SP12/85, 6.
[238] *HMC Salisbury*, XVII, p. 379.
[239] PRO, E351/3232.
[240] Bod. Lib., Rawl. MS D 775, f. 218v.
[241] BL, Add. MS 14044, f. 9r; *HMC Salisbury*, XVII, p. 379.
[242] G. Parnell, 'The Ordnance storehouses in the Tower of London 1450–1700', *Chateau Gaillard* XVIII, p. 171.
[243] 'In the yeare 1501. in the moneth of May, was royall Turney of Lordes and knights in the tower of London before the king', Stow, *Survey of London*, I, p. 58; BL, Egerton MS 2358, f. 12r.
[244] Bod. Lib., Rawl. MS D 776, f. 105r; Rawl. MS D 777, f. 119v.
[245] *L&P*, 1513–14, pp. 1349, 1511, 1512–13; interestingly this building was constructed by the Prior of St Bartholomew's. It may well be that the previous ordnance house had been damaged by the fire of 1512, which had necessitated the reconstruction of the chapel, which also stood on the green.
[246] Bod. Lib., Rawl. MS D 777, f. 119r.
[247] *L&P*, January-June 1536, p. 111.
[248] For example, tilers were employed in 'lathing & Ryppyng as undre pynnyng all the Roffes w^t^ newe Tyle & old Tyle ou^r^ the Ordynnance house Aboue the grene upon the hyll w^t^ in the Tower for safe garde of the kyngs artilleryе & other ordynnes', Bod. Lib., Rawl. MS D 780, f. 245v; see also ff. 255r, 256r. That this was indeed the building constructed in 1514 is further indicated by a payment in 1538 to Sir Christopher Morris, Master of the Ordnance, for 'tiling of other houses of ordnance which the prior of St Bartholomew's heretofore caused to be made', *L&P*, August-December 1538, p. 532.
[249] There is no specific mention of the demolition of the 1514 building, but as that of 1545–7 was clearly in much the same position, it must have happened at this time.
[250] BL, Add. Charter 16334. References later in the century to an external staircase leading up to the armoury perhaps refer to the staircase shown mid-way along the south face of the building on the 1597 survey: PRO, E351/3206; E351/3234.
[251] BL, Add. Charter 16334.
[252] PRO, SP12/22, 15.
[253] There were, of course, other buildings in the Tower used as ordnance stores: a long ordnance house in the 'olde myntt yerde' is referred to in the 1530s, which may have been one of the storehouses described as in the Mint at the end of the century; while a storehouse on Tower Hill was purchased for the department in the 1560s: PRO, E101/474/18; Bod. Lib., Rawl. MS D 776, f. 105r; Rawl. MS D 777, f. 119v; Parnell 'Ordnance storehouses at the Tower of London, 1450–1700', pp. 171–2. The whereabouts of the new house for ordnance for which the Master of Ordnance was paid several hundred pounds in 1538 is unclear, *L&P*, August-December 1538, pp. 527, 532, 535.
[254] *APC*, IV, pp. 323–3. In 1596 one Mr Neville was housed in a room which belonged to the Master of the Ordnance, in June the Lieutenant of the Tower was ordered to move him, *APC*, XXVI, p. 48.
[255] BL, Harl. MS 1326, f. 125r.
[256] J. Haslam, 'Parishes, churches, wards and gates in eastern London', in J. Blair (ed.), *Minsters and Parish Churches: the Local Church in Transition 950–1200* (Oxford, 1988), pp. 35–45.
[257] Colvin (ed.), *The History of the King's Works*, II, pp. 714–15, 722–3.
[258] BL, Egerton MS 2358, ff. 16r, 20r.
[259] Stow, *Survey of London*, I, p. 59.
[260] *L&P*, 1521–3, pp. 1534–5, 1542; PRO, E36/216, ff. 21r, 29v, 31r, 36r.
[261] Bod. Lib., Rawl. MS 775, f. 217v; Rawl. MS D 778, f. 8v.
[262] Bod. Lib., Ashmole MS 862, pp. 299–300.
[263] Bod. Lib., MS Eng Hist e 195, f. 5v.
[264] 'Register of St Peter ad Vincula Tower of London', *passim*. In the mid-1590s, for example, about ten people per year, on average, were buried in the Tower, among them were a Gentleman Porter, a Wardrobe official, the Lieutenant's wife, several prisoners and the chaplain himself.
[265] W. Page (ed.), *Victoria History of London* (London, 1909), pp. 571–2; PRO, SP11/6, f. 55r.
[266] *APC*, XXV, p. 372.
[267] See, for example, *L&P*, 1534, p. 403; *APC*, IV, p. 346; V, p. 33; *The Chronicle of Queen Jane*, p. 27; *CSPD Mary*, p. 150.
[268] B. A. Harrison (ed.), *A Tudor Journal: the Diary of a Priest in the Tower 1580–1585* (London, 2000), p. 40.
[269] Ibid., p. 45.
[270] Colvin (ed.), *The History of the King's Works*, II, p. 713; PRO, WO47/19B, ff. 99v, 105v.
[271] PRO, E101/474/18.
[272] Bod. Lib., Rawl. D 775, ff. 210r, 219v; PRO, E351/3225.
[273] *L&P*, 1534, p. 173.
[274] *The Chronicle of Queen Jane*, p. 27.
[275] BL, Add. MS 34563, f. 7v. There is some ambiguity,

though, about the wording of this: later in the document the word 'aboute' is replaced with 'without'.

[276] PRO, E351/3225; BL, Harl. MS 1326, f. 125r.

[277] PRO, E351/3225.

[278] See, for this and the White Tower in the Tudor period as a whole, the chapters by Roland B. Harris and Anna Keay in E. Impey (ed.), *The White Tower* (forthcoming).

[279] See, for example, *L&P*, 1534, p. 32; PRO, SP12/33, 64; *The Chronicle of Queen Jane*, pp. 42–3; Williams, *Thomas Platter's Travels in England, 1599*, p. 162.

[280] PRO, E101/474/12, f. 4v; E101/474/13, ff. 9–9v.

[281] PRO, E101/474/12, f. 4r; E101/474/13, ff. 1r, 3v.

[282] Bod. Lib., Rawl. MS D 778, ff. 109r–110v; Rawl. MS 780, ff. 246v-251r; Nottingham University Library, Ne. MS 01, May–October 1536.

[283] Bod. Lib., Rawl. MS D 775, f. 204r.

[284] PRO, SP12/47, ff. 35r-36r.

[285] PRO, E351/3202.

[286] PRO, SP12/141, f. 100r.

[287] PRO, SP12/253, f. 69r, this letter refers to the inappropriate conditions in which powder was being kept, which 'was wont ever to bee bestowed into vaults or into the white Tower'.

[288] BL, Add. MS 34,808, f. 139r.

[289] See, for example: PRO, SP1/94, 7; SP14/45, 3.

[290] *John Gerard: the Autobiography of an Elizabethan*, pp. 108–9.

[291] Colvin (ed.), *The History of the King's Works*, II, p. 709; Impey and Parnell, *The Tower of London*, p. 21; Allen Brown and Curnow, *Tower of London*, p. 71.

[292] PRO, E101/474/13, f. 1r.

[293] PRO, E101/474/13, f. 5v.

[294] J. Minsheu, *The Guide into the Tongues* (London, 1617).

[295] This was perhaps the building referred to in 1500–2, which housed the wardrobe of the robes on the top floor and a storehouse on the floor below; BL, Egerton MS 2358, ff. 13r-14r, 16r, 17v-18v.

[296] Parnell, *The Tower of London* (1993), p. 48.

[297] PRO, E101/474/13, f. 2v. Though the distance between the Wardrobe and Broad Arrow towers is slightly more than 101 feet, it is probable that some or all of the old wardrobe building in the area remained when the new building of 1532 was constructed, certainly there is no account for its demolition.

[298] References to the new building of 1532 as a whole only occur in the year of its construction, thereafter the wardrobe of the 'robes' or 'beds' are referred to. Therefore the great doorway mentioned in the new wardrobe of 1532 is presumably the same as that for which great hinges and a great double door were made in the wardrobe of the beds in the following year; Bod. Lib., Rawl. MS D 775, ff. 204r, 217v. A reference from the last year of the century to works on 'halfe a great Roffe of Thoffice of Robes' gives the dimensions of the half roof as 50 foot by 18 foot which is sufficiently close to the dimensions of the new wardrobe of 1532 to suggest they were the same building, PRO, E351/3235.

[299] PRO, E101/474/12, ff. 4r, 5r; E101/474/13, f. 17v.

[300] BL, Egerton MS 2806, ff. 81r, 98r; PRO, LC5/33, f. 87r.

[301] PRO, E101/474/18. Capital letters are used to denote the institution of the Jewel House and lower case its buildings at the Tower.

[302] Bod. Lib., Rawl. MS D 778, *passim.*

[303] Bod. Lib., Rawl. MS D 778, ff. 7r, 8r.

[304] PRO, E36/214, f. 151v.

[305] Bod. Lib., Rawl. MS D 778, ff. 3r, 7r, 8r.

[306] Ibid., f. 99r.

[307] Ibid., f. 101v.

[308] Ibid., f. 109v.

[309] Ibid., ff. 93v, 95r.

[310] Ibid., f. 83v.

[311] Ibid., f. 43r.

[312] Ibid., f. 82r.

[313] Ibid., ff. 49v, 82r.

[314] Ibid., ff. 11r, 98v.

[315] Bod. Lib., Rawl. MS D 775, f. 202r.

[316] Bod. Lib., Rawl. MS D 778, f. 16r.

[317] See A. J. Collins, *The Jewels and Plate of Elizabeth I: the Inventory of 1574* (London, 1955) for the functioning of the Jewel House department.

[318] *CSPD*, 1591–4, p. 3; PRO, E351/3231.

[319] PRO, E351/3211; 3220; 3221; 3223; 3224; 3225; 3233; 3237.

[320] Colvin (ed.), *The History of the King's Works*, II, p. 728. I am grateful to Jeremy Ashbee for sharing with me his extensive work on the great hall in the Middle Ages.

[321] PRO, E101/474/18.

[322] Bod. Lib., Rawl. MS D 775, f. 205r.

[323] Ibid., f. 206r.

[324] Ibid., f. 206r.

[325] Ibid., f. 215r.

[326] Ibid., f. 205r.

[327] Ibid., f. 204r.

[328] Ibid., ff. 210r, 213v, 216v.

[329] Ibid., f. 215r.

[330] Ibid., f. 204r.

[331] Ibid., f. 202r.

[332] Ibid., f. 202r.

[333] Ibid., ff. 204r, 205r.

[334] Hamilton (ed.), *A Chronicle of England*, I, p. 37.

[335] PRO, SP12/3, 46. This verdict was repeated a decade or so later: 'the walles under y$^{e}$ olde hall being sore decayed ... the olde hall is ready to fall downe, the leades therof for the most parte downe, and every day more falling downe'; BL, Add. MS 14044, f. 41v.

[336] PRO, E351/3210.

[337] PRO, E351/3225.

[338] PRO, E351/3238.

[339] PRO, E101/474/18.

[340] PRO, E101/474/12, f. 4r.

[341] PRO, E101/474/13, ff. 1r, 1v. It seems to me that previous readings of these accounts have taken too literally the use of different names for the same chamber: a room might either be described by title (the Queen's great chamber) or by function (the Queen's dining chamber), which should not be taken to prove the existence of two separate chambers.

[342] PRO, E101/474/13, f. 11v.

[343] PRO, E101/474/13, f. 10r.

[344] PRO, E101/474/13, f. 3r.

[345] PRO, E101/474/13, f. 3v.

[346] PRO, E101/474/13, f. 5r.

[347] Bod. Lib., Rawl. MS D 778, f. 73r.

[348] Bod. Lib., Rawl. MS D 778, f. 71v.
[349] PRO, E351/3238.
[350] PRO, E351/3238.
[351] PRO, SP12/22, 15. For the buildings near the jewel house being considered part of the sovereign's apartments in Elizabeth's reign, see PRO, E351/3216.
[352] PRO, E36/214, ff. 23v, 36r, 46v.
[353] Thurley, *The Royal Palaces of Tudor England*, p. 31; J. Schofield, 'City of London gardens, 1500–*c.* 1620', *Garden History* 27, 1 (Summer 1999), pp. 71–87; R. Coope, 'The 'Long Gallery': its origins, development, use and decoration', *Architectural History* 29 (1986), pp. 44–84.
[354] Thurley, *The Royal Palaces of Tudor England*, p. 137.
[355] PRO, E101/474/12, f. 5r.
[356] PRO, E101/474/12, f. 5v.
[357] Ibid.
[358] Ibid.
[359] *L&P*, August-December 1541, p. 670.
[360] *L&P*, August-December 1541, p. 671.
[361] *L&P*, 1542, p. 675; BL, Add. MS 10109, f. 173r.
[362] *APC*, IV, p. 323.
[363] BL, Add. MS 34563, f. 7r.
[364] PRO, E351/3219.
[365] PRO, E351/3231; *CSPD*, 1595–7, pp. 265, 267.
[366] It was to here, the room 'in the side of the gallery', that Thomas Seymour was called by the Privy Council in February 1549 to answer the charges of treason levelled against him; *APC*, II, p. 247.
[367] *APC*, II, pp. 12, 22, 28, 29, 34. Between 1542 and 1600 the Privy Council met at the Tower of London on only a few occasions at the beginning of each reign: 1, 2, 6, 7, 12, 13 and 15 February 1547; 23 February 1549; 13, 14, 16, 29 August and 29 September 1553; 18 January 1554; 30 November, 1, 3, 4 December 1558 and 14 January 1559: see entries in *APC*, II, IV, V, VII.
[368] *APC*, II, pp. 7–8.
[369] *APC*, II, pp. 8–9.
[370] 'As I told you in the gallery at the Tower the day after the king first came there ...', *Calendar of State Papers Domestic Series of the reign of Edward VI 1547–1553*, ed. C. S. Knighton (London, 1992), p. 121.
[371] Colvin (ed.), *The History of the King's Works*, II, pp. 711, 725; Thurley, 'Royal lodgings at the Tower of London', pp. 37, 54–6.
[372] BL, Egerton MS 2358, ff. 15r-20r. The accounts are less descriptive about the position of the King's bedchamber in Henry VIII's reign than in his father's. But when it is considered that both the Lanthorn Tower as well as the small tower to its south are being described in the reference of 1532 to 'the new tow$^{r}$ at the west ende of the kynges gallery over the kynges bedechamb$^{r}$ and prevy closset', and that the Lanthorn Tower was still the site of the King's bedchamber in the seventeenth century, PRO, E351/3259, it can only be concluded that the bedchamber did not move from the Lanthorn Tower position in the sixteenth century.
[373] This is suggested on the basis that there was 'a doore comyng of the same chamber into the ledys'; PRO, E101/474/13, f. 9v.
[374] Thurley, *The Royal Palaces of Tudor England*, p. 142.
[375] Construction of the new building began in the summer preceding the long-awaited arrival of Catherine of Aragon in England and it may be that the use of the Tower by the young couple (before Prince Arthur's premature death) was anticipated; PRO, E101/415, ff. 60v, 70r, 74r, 86v.
[376] The key visual source for deciphering this most complex part of the Tower of London is a collection of eighteenth-century plans in the PRO, the most important being WORK 31/182, 183 and 186. These indicate that the new tower had a floor at the level of, and connecting with, the wall-walk and another over that which sat on top of the outer curtain wall.
[377] PRO, E101/474/13, f. 12v. Henry VII instituted the formal office of the King's Library, and the library at Richmond was shown with great pride during the festivities of Prince Arthur's wedding; G. Kipling, 'Henry VII and the origins of Tudor patronage', in G. F. Lytle and S. Orgel (eds.), *Patronage in the Renaissance* (Princeton, 1981) pp. 117–64; Thurley, *The Royal Palaces of Tudor England*, p. 141.
[378] '... takyng downe of the olde selynges and shelves in the kynges prevy chambre that now is made before kyng henry the vii library', PRO, E101/474/13, f. 12r.
[379] PRO, E101/474/13, f. 11v.
[380] Ibid., f. 12r.
[381] Ibid., f. 11v.
[382] The medieval Lanthorn Tower was demolished in 1776 — the 'Lanthorn Tower' standing today was built in the 1880s.
[383] The assertion in Colvin (ed.), *The History of the King's Works*, III, p. 266 that all the buildings of the royal apartments were demolished in the seventeenth century is incorrect, much of the royal lodgings survived — albeit often in an altered form — until the late eighteenth century.
[384] See note 341 above. In contemporary accounts the 'great' and 'great watching' chambers were often the same room in a palace, as were the 'presence' and 'dining' chambers; Thurley, *The Royal Palaces of Tudor England*, pp. 120, 122. Much confusion about the layout of the royal palace in the Tower has stemmed from a misunderstanding of this.
[385] PRO, E101/474/18.
[386] PRO, E101/474/13, f. 1r.
[387] PRO, E101/474/13, f. 1v.
[388] Bod. Lib., Rawl. MS D 775, f. 206r.
[389] The entrance to the great watching chamber was provided with 'a penthous over the hed of it for y$^{e}$ wether' PRO, E101/474/13, f. 1v. It seems that beneath the principal room of this building was a cellar of Caen and Reigate stone; in 1532 repairs were carried out to 'wyndowes on the syde undernethe the watchechamber to geve light into the sellar', E101/474/13, f. 9v.
[390] PRO, SP12/3, 46.
[391] PRO, E101/474/13, f. 5r.
[392] Ibid., f. 9v.
[393] PRO, E101/474/12, ff. 5r, 12v.
[394] PRO, E101/474/13, f. 11v.
[395] Bod. Lib., Rawl. MS D 775, f. 218r.
[396] PRO, WORK 31/183, 182.
[397] For this building, which was altered to house the administrative offices of the Ordnance Office in 1672–3, being composed of pre-existing structures see G. Parnell, 'The Tower of London: The Reconstruction of the Inmost Ward

during the reign of Charles II', *Transactions of the London and Middlesex Archaeological Society*, XXXI (1980), p. 154 and *The Tower of London* (1993), p. 67.
[398] PRO, E101/474/13, f. 2r.
[399] The southern chamber was that which Simon Thurley suggested was the Queen's hall in the thirteenth century; Thurley, 'Royal lodgings at the Tower of London 1216–1327', pp. 36–57.
[400] Hamilton (ed.), *A Chronicle of England*, I, pp. 180–1.
[401] *CSPD Mary*, pp. 9–10.
[402] After her coronation, Elizabeth seems never to have spent a night at the Tower; indeed when she visited the castle in 1561 she spent the night at Lord North's house in Smithfield, instead: *CSPD*, 1601–3, p. 513.
[403] PRO, SP12/22, no. 15.
[404] BL, Add. MS 34563, f. 7r.
[405] BL, Add. MS 10,109, f. 173r-v.
[406] BL, Harl. MS 1326, f. 125r.
[407] Jeremy Ashbee, 'A mediaeval garden at the Tower of London', *The London Gardener* V (1999–2000), pp. 11–14.
[408] Bod. Lib., Rawl. MS D 775, f. 219v.
[409] PRO, E101/474/13, f. 10v.
[410] PRO, E101/474/13, f. 2v.
[411] PRO, E101/474/13, ff. 2v, 5r.
[412] BL, Egerton MS 2358, ff. 14r, 16r, 20r; Harl. MS 1326, f. 125r; Add. MS 34563.
[413] PRO, E101/474/13, f. 2r. This, 'a new bridge w$^{t}$ out the Tower next seint Kateryns whiche comes into the quenes garden', might indicate something which gave access into the Queen's garden over the curtain wall(s), but could also refer to a structure leading down into the garden from the Well Tower.
[414] PRO, E101/474/12, ff. 2r, 4v, 10v; in the King's garden 23 square timber steps were 'sett abowte the new bridge'.
[415] PRO, E101/474/13, f. 10v.
[416] BL, Add. MS 14044, f. 9r. D. Jacques, 'The *compartiment* system in Tudor England', *Garden History* 27:1 (Summer 1999), pp. 32–53. The low brick walls in the Whitehall privy garden are famously visible in the background of the anonymous painting of *The Family of Henry VIII.*
[417] *APC*, IV, p. 59.
[418] *The Chronicle of Queen Jane*, p. 33. BL, Add. MS 34563. Interestingly, the Dudley brothers were also granted this freedom, making it entirely possible, contrary to what is sometimes argued, that Elizabeth and Robert Dudley's paths could have crossed when they were imprisoned at the Tower; *APC*, IV, p. 379, cf. S. Doran, *Monarchy and Matrimony: the Courtships of Elizabeth I* (London and New York, 1996), p. 40.
[419] *APC*, IV, p. 379.
[420] BL, Add. MS 14044, f. 41r-v.
[421] Even the view of London by Hollar, published in 1647, shows vegetation in this part of the Tower.
[422] PRO, E351/3216; 3228; *John Gerard: the Autobiography of an Elizabethan*, p. 132. Among the works done at the Tower in 1600–1 was the mending of the floor of 'a prison in the previe garden'; PRO, E351/3236.
[423] It seems that the Haiward and Gascoyne survey may have been a little more instructive in this respect than now appears: when examined under ultra-violet light, the Whitehand copy indicates that the garden areas were given a wash of some sort which is no longer visible; the Lieutenant's garden, the privy and great gardens, parts of the Nine Gardens and the churchyard of All Hallows were all treated in this way. A pathway running between the doorway in the building across the north end of the great garden and the gateway under the gallery can also be clearly seen in ultra-violet light.
[424] Colvin (ed.), *The History of the King's Works*, II, pp. 726–7.
[425] It may be that these were placed in the western section of the wharf to keep them out of sight of the royal lodgings; certainly this was the reason given for the abandoning of a scheme to erect a crane in the eastern half in 1611; BL, Add. MS 14044, f. 36r.
[426] It is clear that private agents did not always adhere to the regulations forbidding them to land goods at the Tower wharf; *APC*, II, p. 301, see also BL, Add. MS 14044, f. 36r.
[427] Parnell, 'Ordnance storehouses at the Tower of London, 1450–1700', p. 171.
[428] *L&P*, 1534, p. 399. Sir John Peyton complained of the assignment of these houses to the Master of the Armoury, and suggested that they should instead be leased out by the crown directly; Bod. Lib., MS Eng Hist e 195, f. 3r-v.
[429] *CSPD Mary I*, p. 121.
[430] *L&P*, 1546–7, p. 448.
[431] PRO, SP12/3, 46; BL, Add. MS, 14044, f. 40r.
[432] PRO, E351/3202.
[433] PRO, E351/3209.
[434] Ibid.
[435] PRO, E351/3212.
[436] The officers of the Tower blamed the state of the wharf on the wear it received from the shipping of ordnance there, and it may be that the need to repair it within twenty years of the works of the 1570s was due to the significant increase in military activity in the later years of Elizabeth's reign; *CSPD*, 1591–4, p. 515.
[437] PRO, E351/3227.
[438] PRO, E351/3227; 3228.
[439] Ibid.
[440] BL, Lansdowne MS 76, f. 77r.
[441] The wall was built as the estimate anticipated: the first section was 'from the ende of the wall by the wardehouse to the watergate', the accounts then record 'continewinge and finishinge the foresaid Brickwall from the wardehouse and watergate alonge towardes S$^{t}$ Katherins gate', PRO, E351/3229.
[442] *L&P*, 1534, p. 178; *John Gerard: the Autobiography of an Elizabethan*, pp. 130–5.
[443] PRO, SP12/189, 11.
[444] PRO, SP12/157, 53. BL, Add. MS 14044, f. 40r.
[445] *John Gerard: the Autobiography of an Elizabethan,* p. 135.
[446] PRO, E351/3230, 3231.
[447] Some idea of the grandeur and popularity of these occasions is given by the painting of *The arrival of the Venetian ambassador at the Tower stairs, May 1707* by Luca Carlevaris.
[448] 'against the landinge of Thambassador of Denmarke', PRO, E351/3232.
[449] *CSPD*, 1598–1601, p. 602. The works in the last five years of the reign included the laying of ashlar hard stone on the wharf and stairs and extensive repairs to the sluices; see Colvin (ed.), *The History of the King's Works*, III, pp. 271–2 for a discussion of this. PRO, E351/3235; 3236; 3237.

# VII. APPENDICES

**APPENDIX A**

**ROYAL ARMOURIES, MS I. 243**

October: 1597
A declaracon of the state of yo[r] Highnes Tower of London at such tyme as it pleased yo[r] Ma:[tie] to commaund mee yo[r] Highnes most humble, Loyall, devoted servaunt, unto the service of the same, under the guarde wherof there is conteyned as ffolloweth

First yo[r] Ma:[ties] Royall Stores of Amunytions for warre, w[th] the dangerous Charge of yo[r] Highnes Magasynes of Powder
Secondly, yo[r] Ma:[ties] rich Treasures, of Jewells, Plate, and furnytures
Thirdly, yo[r] Highnes Recordes
ffourthly, the office of the Mynte
fffifthly, the Prysoners for causes of state
The place it self (under the guarde wherof, these yo[r] Ma:[ties] Royall stores and rich Treasures etc, are conteyned) beeing under the charge and commande of the (capten and) Lieutennt, whose office and dutye (by Presydent of former tymes) seemeth to consist of three p̲ts.

| | |
|---|---|
| | Millitary |
| Viz | Justiciary |
| | Pollitique |

The Millitary parte consisteth in Judicyall discerninge the state of the place, how it standeth seated, guarded, and Munyted for defence, And in what sorte weakened, by decayes, disorders, or other defects, and what may bee added for the better safetye of the same.
To governe and commaund the guarde, and such others, as by yo[r] Ma:[tie] shalbee Appoynted in their Assistaunce, for the better strengthening of yo[r] service in this place, under a Martiall and civill Rule of disciplyne and obedyence.
And fynally, To Mannage and dispose all things, app̲teyning unto the safetye and defence of this yo[r] Highnes Royal Castell. In such sorte, as may best stande w[th] the securitye therof.

The Justiciary parte, is civilly to governe, and Reteyne in good correspondence of Obedyence and Peace, Aswell the officers and warders appoynted for the guarde of the place, as allso other p̲sonns Resydinge w[th]in the Lyberties of this government.
To Restrayne and punishe all Insolencyes, vyolencyes, and disorders, The w[ch] are nowe in this Latter, contentious, and disobedyent Age, exceedinglye Mulltyplyed: Smale offences suffered (in this place) may suddenlye prove great dangers, and therfore necessary to bee Quenched and Suppressed in the smoake, beefore they come to the furye of flame, The Reforming power and Justiciarye Aucthority of the Lieuetennt in such cases is (by dicontynuance) grown doubtfull, w[ch] may in some sorte prove Inconvenyent.

The Pollitique parte is to discerne and Apprehend, the sufficiencye, dilligence, dutye and Loyall Obedyence of all officers, and other p̲sons app̲teyninge to this place, or Resyding w[th]in this Charge, or the Lybertyes therof.
To hould good Correspondence, in all yo[r] Highnes services, w[th] all the seid officers, and other p̲sonns, and allso w[th] the confyninge Lybertyes of the cittye of London.
And fynally to discover the Nature, disposition, pollicye, dependencye, and Practize, of all such as shalbee (for cause of offence agaynst yo[r] Ma:[ties] p̲son or state) deteyned under handes of Restraynt.

These (most gratious Sovereigne) beeing necessarye and dependent dutyes to bee expected from him, unto whom yo[r] Highnes shall comitte the charge of so high a trust (beeing in these practizing and conspiring tymes of more Importance then ever) doe enforce mee, (out of the true discoverye of myne imp̲fections) most humbly and truly to Confesse, That this place Requyreth a person of farre better parts and judgement, then standeth w[th] my habilitye to p̲forme, Notw[th]standing, to supply some part of my wants, I will Add a Loyall dutye, and dilligent Indevour, w[th]out any dependencye, ende, or other Respect, But onlye upon yo[r] Sacred person, and to doe yo[r] Highnes all faythfull and Loyall Service.

In these Respects, I have presumed to present unto yo[r] most excellent Ma:[tie] The plotte and declaracon of the state of this yo[r] Highnes Tower, and Castell Royall, Togeather w[th] the differences, defects, and dangers, necessary to bee reformed concerninge the same, as followeth

Differences Necessary to bee decyded

Inprimis The cittye of London did and doth pretend Title, unto yo[r] Ma:[ties] soyle of Tower hill, (and Eastsmithfield) even unto the ditch of the Tower, and allso unto diverse houses at the Posterne gate, and at the Bullwarcke, The possession wherof, hath allwayes been in yo[r] Ma:[tie]

To Admitte of this their Challenge were dangerous and Inconvenyent unto the safety of the place, By Couller wherof The Cittyzens of London should have power to make their Muster even at the Tower ditch, and allso their disordered Mulltytudes of Artificers, Journeymen, and Prentyzes, (by whose Insolencyes in former tymes, offence unto the peace of the state hath been often offered) might at their pleasure assemble uppon the counterscarpe of the ditch, from whence they may passe (w[th] Little impeachment) to the walles of the Tower, The ditch beeing at this present in many parts decayed and passable, and the walles in some places easye to bee mounted.

All manner of Assemblyes neare the counterscarpe of any castell or cittadell, are by Pollicye and Martiall disciplyne utterly restrayned, And therfore of purpose, before all such Royall defences, A spatious place of view is ever lefte playn and unbuilded, to the Intente, the capteyne and guarde that have charge of the same, might the better discerne any Approach or Attempte intended, And from the w$^{ch}$ place in dangerous tymes all concourse and Troupings of People are to bee Inhibited.

If yo$^{r}$ Highnes should suffer this pretended Intrusion and incroachment upon the Auntient Lybertyes of yo$^{r}$ Ma$^{ties}$ Castell Royall, Then followeth this Inconvenyence, That if yo$^{r}$ Ma:$^{tie}$ in yo$^{r}$ Princely Provydence and wysedome for the better defence and safety of this place, (yo$^{r}$ Highnes Magasynes of Amunytions and Treasures heerin conteyned beeing of high and Inestymable consequence) shall determyne, to make any Royall or p̱fect fortification: The soyle and onlye place of Advantage for that purpose, shalbee (by Couller and Prextext of the cittyes Right) w$^{th}$drawne and detracted.

Yo$^{r}$ Ma:$^{ties}$ Princely pleasure touching this Question (of yo$^{r}$ Highnes Right and Prerogative Royall) beeing signified, wilbee a meanes of unyon and good correspondence, to bee held in all yo$^{r}$ Highnes services beetwixt the Citty and those, unto whose Trust yo$^{r}$ Highnes shall comitt the charge of this place.

Defectes, Needfull to bee supplyed

Item Ther are Allowed for the guarde of this yo$^{r}$ Ma:$^{ties}$ Royall Castell, but Thirtye warders, wherof, there doe but fower keepe the whole nights watche (w$^{th}$out Releeving) five nights in the weeke, And five thother two nights, beeing nothinge sufficient nor proportionable, consydering the Largenes of the place, w$^{ch}$ conteyneth by the counterscarp of the ditch Three Hundredth paces, under the guarde wherof ther is allso conteyned, yo$^{r}$ Ma:$^{ties}$ store of Munytion and Powder, Treasure, of Jewells and Plate etc: Allso the Prysoners of great charge, All w$^{ch}$ Lying disp̱sed in many places, cannot bee safelye guarded, w$^{th}$ so weake a watche.

To these thirty warders, yo$^{r}$ Highnes doth allowe but eight pence a peece p̱ diem, the w$^{ch}$ sufficeth not to feede them above one meale in a daye, In Respect wherof, such as doe Resyde upon the service, are enforced to help themselves by watching and warding for other their fellowes, who followe their trades and pryvate busynes, and some (havinge double offices) attend in other places, By occasion wherof, The place is ever unfurnished of two parts of the weake guarde beelonging to the same.

Yo$^{r}$ Ma:$^{tie}$ hath in paye seven score gunners, and twenty Labourers, The gunners have in former tymes watched certein of them every night, but by sufferance this service hath been discontynewed, and yet necessary to bee observed, In Regarde of yo$^{r}$ Ma:$^{ties}$ Powder and Munytion being under the Charge of that Office.

The labourers allso, whose Labours beeing but seeldome and easye, may (if it is so stande w$^{th}$ yo$^{r}$ Princely pleasure) bee enioyned to strengthen the watch w$^{th}$ (every night) three, Soe as they observing turnes should watch but one night in a weeke.

All other Inhabitants what soever, dwelling w$^{th}$in the Tower or the Lyberties of the same, may by equall proportion observe their turnes in watching, In Respect they are Pryvielieged from all service in other places.

Ther are allso by Anntient Presydents (the w$^{ch}$ have been Contynewed sithens yo$^{r}$ Ma:$^{ties}$ most happy Reigne) dyverse hambletts, as Stratford Hackney, Shordich and others beelonging unto the Tower, who have (upon Occasion of commaund) given their attendaunce, both to watch and guarde this yo$^{r}$ Ma:$^{ties}$ Royall Castell, In Respect wherof, they have ever been freed from Muster out of their owne Lybertyes, and from charge and Impresting into fforreigne services.

Disorders Meete to bee Reformed

Item It hath beene suffered, That all Prysoners havinge the Lybertye of the Tower, might have contynuall accesse of all manner of persons unto them w$^{th}$out nomber, or any Notice taken of their names, or Occasions of Repayre A thinge most dangerous in Respecte of the small guarde, allowed for the keeping of a place of such consequence, and not possible (allowinge so great a concourse of People) to Restrayne the Trayterous Prysoners from Intelligence and Practize.

It hath allso been p̱mitted, That all p̱sonns coming unto a Prysoner having the Lybertye of the Tower, might Contynew w$^{th}$ him in his chamber or ellse where in meale tymes, and in tymes of devyne service, The gates of the Tower beeing then shutte, and the guarde therof Retyred, The w$^{ch}$ may geve Occasion of great Inconvenyence.

Allso Prysoners havinge the Lyberty of the Tower, have been allowed to keepe their wyves and whole famylyes there Resydent, (The w$^{ch}$ by former tolleracon doth still contynew) All w$^{ch}$ in meale tymes and in tymes of devyne service, have had lyberty w$^{th}$in the Tower at their pleasure the danger wherof is humbly Referred unto yo$^{r}$ Highnes consideracon etc.

Lykewyse the warders and other p̱sonns dwelling w$^{th}$in the Tower, have used to keepe their famylyes, (viz their wyves Chilldren and servanntes) w$^{th}$in the same, w$^{ch}$ is Occasion of great Repayre, and dangerous in Regarde of the Powder, and for Intelligence to the Prysoners etc.

Allso the warders, Minters, and other the Inhabitants, have usually lodged their their ffreindes and other strangers w$^{th}$ in the Tower, w$^{th}$ out any Allowance of the Lieutennt, or Notice therof given unto him.

Ther hath (allso) been suffered a comon Brewhowse and Backhowse to bee kept w$^{th}$in the Mynte, and allso a Comon Hackney stable to Leat horses to hyre, who have had their Contynnuall passage (w$^{th}$ their Caryage and horses) in and out at the great gates, w$^{ch}$ (beeing very disgracefull and Inconvenyent) I have Restrayned.

The Inhabitanntes upon the wharfe, the Bullwarcke, and the Posterne have Landed upp the Tower ditch on their backesydes, and dyverse of them have built noysome places in the same, By meanes wherof, the ditch is in many places utterly decayed, and the water corrupted, the Lyke is allso done by the Inhabitanntes of S$^{t}$: Katherynes

Yo$^{r}$ Ma:$^{ties}$ Lodgings and many other Buildings w$^{th}$ in the Tower, are in decaye and may bee in tyme Repayred w$^{th}$ smale charge, beeing well surveyed and provydently bestowed

Allso the auntient slewces and vaulltes that were wonte to bee maynteyned, to take in water out of the Thames, for strengthening of the Tower ditch, are nowe utterly decayed.

There are allso diverse Tennements of Late tymes buillded, w$^{th}$ in the Lybertye of the Tower, By meanes wherof, the Inhabitants are soe encreased as there is not w$^{th}$in the Tower, any place sufficient for their Buryalls, The w$^{ch}$, in tymes of Infection wilbee moste dangerous, and in other Respects very Inconvenyent.

If it seeme good unto yo$^{r}$ most excellent Ma:$^{tie}$ That these Orders might bee Considered, the defects viewed, and in yo$^{r}$ Princely wysedome the Remedyes added, It wilbee a great addition unto the defence and safe keeping of this yo$^{r}$ Highnes Royall Castell, the Munytions Treasures and Prysone$^{rs}$ therin remayninge, and a Comforte unto such yo$^{r}$ Ma:$^{ties}$ Loyall Subiects unto whose trust the charge of the same shalbee comitted, Beeinge now by Occasions of these decayes, weake guardes, former Tolleracons and disorders so full of ffeares, dangers, and Infynite Accydents of displeasure, As no Man beeing Loyally devoted unto yo$^{r}$ sacred service but must tremble in dismaye of his contynuance in yo$^{r}$ Highnes favour (beeing in all submisse humblenes and devoted Loyallty) more desired then all other earthly happynes whatsoever

Y$^{r}$ ma$^{tyes}$
moste humble and loyall seruant
S John Peyton

## APPENDIX B

## BODLEIAN LIBRARY, MS ENG. HIST. E. 195

A Declaration of the state of the Tower of London at suche tyme as it pleased your Ma$^{tie}$ to commaunde me (yo$^{r}$ Highnes moste humble, loyall, devoted servant) unto the service of the same, under the guarde wherof there is conteined, as followeth

firste, yo$^{r}$ Mat:$^{ies}$ royall stores of ammunition for warr, w$^{th}$ the dangerous chardge of your Highnes magasines of powder.

Secondly, yo$^{r}$ Ma$^{ts}$ ritch treasure, of jewells, plate and furnitures.
Thirdly, your highnes records.
ffourthly, the office of the mynte:
ffyftly the prysoners for causes of State:

The place it self under the guarde wherof, thes yo$^{r}$ Ma$^{ts}$ royall stores & ritch treasures &c$^{a}$ conteyned, under y$^{e}$ chardge & conduct of y$^{e}$ capten & Lieutennte whose office & dutie (by precedent of former tymes) seemeth to consist of three parts.

viz Millitarie
Justiciare
Politique

The millitarie ꝑte consisteth in judiciall discerninge the state of y$^{e}$ place, howe it standeth seated, guarded and munited for defence, and in what sorte weakned by decayes disorders or defects & what maie bee added for y$^{e}$ better safetie of the same:

To governe & comaunde y$^{e}$ garde, & suche others as by yo$^{r}$ ma$^{tie}$ shalbee appoynted in their assistance for y$^{e}$ better strengthninge of yo$^{r}$ service in this place, under a martiall & civil rule of discipline & obedience.
And finally to mannage & dispose all things apperteyninge unto y$^{e}$ safetie & defence of this yo$^{r}$ Highnes royall castell in suche sorte as maie best stand w$^{th}$ y$^{e}$ securitie therof.

The Justiciarie parte, is Civilly to governe and reteyne in good corespondence of obedience & peace aswell y$^{e}$ officers and warders appoynted for y$^{e}$ guard of y$^{e}$ place; As also all other ꝑsons residinge w$^{th}$ in y$^{e}$ liberties of this goverment.
To restrayne & punnishe all insolencies, violencies and disorders, y$^{e}$ w$^{ch}$ are nowe in this latter, contentious & disobedient age exceedingly multeplied. Smale offence suffred in y$^{s}$ place, maie suddenly prove great dangers, and therfore necessary to bee quenched & suppressed in the smoake, before they come to y$^{e}$ fury of flame.

> The reforminge power and justiciare aucthoritie of the Lieutenant in suche cases is by discontinuance growne doubtfull, whiche maie in some sorte prove inconvenient.

The Politique parte is to discerne & apprehend the sufficiencie, dilligence, dutie & loyall obedience of all officers and other ꝑsons apperteyninge to y$^{s}$ place or residinge w$^{th}$ in this chardge or the liberties therof.
To holde good corespondence in all yo$^{r}$ highnes services w$^{th}$ all the said officers & other ꝑsons and also w$^{th}$ the confininge liberties of y$^{e}$ Citie of London.
And finally to discover the nature, disposition, pollicye dependency and practize of al suche as shalbee (for cause of offence agaynst yo$^{r}$ Highnes personne or State) deteyned under bands of restraynt.

> Theis moste gratious Soveraigne (beinge necessarie & dependant duties to be expected from him, unto whome your Highnes shall

comitt the charge of so high a trust beinge in theis practisinge and conspiringe tymes of more importance then ever) do enforce mee out of the true discoverie of mine owne imperfections, moste humbly to confess, that this place requireth a parson of farr better parts and judgement, then standeth w$^{th}$ my habilitie to performe. Notwithstandinge to suply some parte of my wants; I will add a loyal dutie and diligent indever, w$^{th}$ out any dependency, end or other respects, but only upon your sacred personne, and to doe your Ma:$^{tie}$ all faithfull & loiall service.

Differences necessarie to bee decided.
Inprimis, The Cittie of London did and dothe pretend title unto your Ma$^{ts}$ soyle of Tower hill & east Smithfield even unto y$^{e}$ ditche of the Tower, and also unto divers houses at the posterne gate, and at y$^{e}$ Bulwarke The possession wherof hath alwaies byn in yo$^{r}$ Ma:$^{tie}$

To admit of this their challendge weare dangerous and inconvenient unto y$^{e}$ safetie of the place, By couller wherof y$^{e}$ Citezens of London should have power to make their Muster even at the Tower ditche; and also their disordred multitudes of artificers, Journeymen & prentices (by whose insolencies in former tymes offence unto y$^{e}$ peace of the state hath byn often offred) might at y$^{ier}$ pleasure assemble upon the Counterscarpe of y$^{e}$ ditch: ffrom whence they maye passe (w$^{th}$ litle impeachem$^{t}$) to y$^{e}$ walles of y$^{e}$ Tower, the ditch beinge at this present in manie ꝑts decayed and passable, and y$^{e}$ walls in some places easie to bee mounted.

All manner of assemblies, neare y$^{e}$ Counterscarpe of anie Castell or Citadell, are by pollicie & martiall disciplyne utterly restrayned; And therfore (of purpose before all suche Royall defences a spacious place of viewe is ever left playne and unbuilded, to y$^{e}$ entend y$^{e}$ Capten & garde y$^{t}$ have chardge of y$^{e}$ same might y$^{e}$ better discerne anie approche or attempt intended; and from y$^{e}$ w$^{ch}$ place (in dangerous tymes) all concourse & troupinges of people are to bee inhibited.

Yf yo$^{r}$ highnes should suffer this pretended intrusion and incrochement upon y$^{e}$ antient liberties of yo$^{r}$ Ma$^{ts}$ Castle royall then follow$^{th}$ this inconvenience, y$^{t}$ if your Ma:$^{tie}$ in your pryncely providence & wisdome for y$^{e}$ better defence & safety of this place, yo$^{r}$ Ma$^{ts}$ magasyns of amunitions & treasures herin remayninge beinge of high and inestimable consequence shall determyn to make anie royall or ꝑfect fortification: the soyle & only place of advantage for y$^{t}$ purpose, shalbe (by Couller & pretext of y$^{e}$ Citties right) w$^{th}$drawne and detracted.

For decidinge of this antient and inconvenient controversy touchinge the Tower liberties and priveleges, your Ma$^{tie}$ hath graunted a comission to the Judges, unto whome I have delivered apparant proofes for your Highnes title, upon whose reporte your Ma$^{ts}$: princely pleasure touchinge this question (of yo$^{r}$ Highnes right & prerogative royall) beinge signefied, will be a meanes of union and good corespondence to bee held (in all your Highnes services) betwixt the cittie and those, unto whose trust your Highnes shall comitt the chardge of this place.

Ther is also of late some difference betwene the Lieutenant and y$^{e}$ M$^{r}$ Porter, touchinge y$^{e}$ Jurisdiction and orderinge of y$^{e}$ wharf: In w$^{ch}$ y$^{e}$ Gent porter intrudeth upon y$^{e}$ authoritie of y$^{e}$ Lieutenant, confoundinge therby the iurisdiction of place and dutye of office.

The wharf beinge a speciall part of the fortification of the Tower, the order and iurisdiction therof (as in all defensive place of the like nature) doth belong unto y$^{e}$ commaunder of the place no other officer beinge therin interessed further; then to execute suche direction, as for your Ma$^{ties}$ service shalbee commaunded, The which is also proved by your Ma$^{ties}$ records.

The houses upon y$^{e}$ Eastend of y$^{e}$ wharf & under London wall, are challendged by y$^{e}$ Master of y$^{e}$ Armory; And the houses upon y$^{e}$ west end of y$^{e}$ wharf, at y$^{e}$ Bulwark, the posterne and y$^{e}$ watergate by the Gentleman Porter, as apperteyninge to their offices; w$^{ch}$ have byn in former tymes (by yo$^{r}$ Ma$^{ts}$ moste noble progenitors) demised unto the warders, officers and artificers belonginge unto the Tower, But of late inhabited by Strangers manie of them beinge very poore & disordred persons, by meanes wherof contentions & quarrells are daily moved: Of theis houses therare fower score builded synce y$^{e}$ tyme of your Ma$^{ts}$ moste happie raigne, and manie of them in places inconvenient.

Theis houses beinge wourth 200$^{li}$ per Annu are generally conceved to be in your Ma$^{ts}$ disposition, and neither graunted nor belonging unto anie office, or other personne; It weare therfore a great advancement unto your service & to the peacable gouverment and safetie of this place, to have the saide houses inhabited by you Ma:$^{ts}$ immediat Tennants without anie termes graunted, but at your Highnes pleasure, whoe might bee enioyned to strengthen the watche, and to performe all other necessarie duties; And yet notw$^{th}$standinge your Ma:$^{tie}$ might of your bountie, allowe unto the M$^{r}$ of the Armoury and M$^{r}$ Porter out of the farmes of the said houses, as great a benefit as thy doe at this present receave.

Defects needfull to bee suplied.
Item ther are allowed for y$^{e}$ guard of this your Ma$^{ts}$ royall, Castell but 30 warders, wherof ther are but fower keepe the whole nighte watche (w$^{th}$out releevinge) five nights in the weeke; and five the other two nights, beinge nothinge sufficient nor proportionable; consideringe the largenes of the place; w$^{ch}$ conteyneth by the Counter Scarpe of the ditche 693 paces; Under the guard wherof ther is also conteyned yo$^{r}$ Ma$^{ts}$ store of munition & powder, treasure of Jewells and plate &c$^{a}$. Also y$^{e}$ prisoners of great chardge. All w$^{ch}$ (beinge dispersed in divers places) cannot bee safely guarded w$^{th}$ so weake a watche.

To theis 30 warders, yo$^{r}$ Ma$^{tie}$ dothe allowe but viii$^{d}$ a peece ꝑ diem in respect of w$^{ch}$ smale wages regardinge the deernes of theis tymes, wherin the prices of all things and all mens labors are increased they are growne to exceedinge povertie; And those moste poore, that best attend your Ma[ts] service.

> Your Highnes yomen of the great chamber have twice tasted of your Princely bountie by advancinge their wages; Theis poore mens travells exceedinge all other your Highnes servants, doe merite commisseration, the whiche out of compassion, I humbly remember to your Ma[ties] good pleasure.

Ther bee amongst y[e] warders divers unfitt for the place; some of them utterly neglectinge their duties in service, others given to druncknes, disorders and quarrells, other for debilitie of bodye unable to pforme their duties, others double officed and cannot attend in two places. By meanes whereof, the guarde of this place is muche weakned.

> In this you [*sic*] Ma:[ts] pleasure is humbly desired.

Yo[r] Ma[tie] by Bill assigned hath graunted divers warders romes in reversion, and divers other are to bee presented unto yo[r] highnes, manie of the pties beinge unfitt for y[e] place: The manner of yo[r] Ma[ts] graunt by those Bills is for terme of lief, by means wherof suche as are founde negligent, unable or unfaithfull in yo[r] service cannot bee by course of law dischardged

> It maie therfore pleas your Ma:[tie] to graunt those romes ad bene placitum, and for for lief; whiche wilbee an occasion to keepe the warders in better regarde of their duties, & more dilligent in your Highnes seruice.

Yo[r] Ma[tie] hath in paye divers officers & arteficers belonginge unto the ordennce; and also 140 Gunners and 20 laborers all w[ch] ought to watch and warde in the Tower.

> Proved by establishment 25[o] Julii An[o]. 1 H.8.

The xx[th] of October Ano.3. H.8. S[r] Thomas Seymor knight then beinge M[r] of the Ordennce, Sir Thomas Arrundell and S[r] Robert Terwitt Comissioners of the said ordennce, composition was by them made that y[e] officers, artificers and gunners should paye certen money in dischardge of the said service.

> Proved by the order signed by the said S[r] Thos: Seymor

All inhabitants whatsoever, dwellinge w[th] in y[e] Tower or the liberties of y[e] same, maie by equall proporcon observe their turnes in watchinge, in respect they are priveledged from all service in other places.

Ther are also by antient precedent (the w[ch] have byn contynued synce your Ma[ts] moste happie raigne) xvii hamblets belonging unto y[e] Tower, viz: S[t] Katherens, Eastsmithfield, Stepney, Ratclif, Lymehouse, Blackwall, Mile end, Bednall greene, Stoke newingtonn, Hackney, Branley, Finsbury cum memb: white chappell, Hoggsdon, Shorditch, Norton folgate and Stratforde on the Bowe. All theis have upon occasion of commaunde given their attendaunce both to watche & guarde this your Ma[ts] royall Castell, in respect wherof they have ever byn freed from muster out of their owne liberties, and from certen other extraordenary Chardges.

Theis priviledges have byn infringed by the iustices of midd, wherby the hamblets hold them selves freed from their antient service, by the w[ch] they weare by custome bounde, w[t] out anie paye or chardge unto your Ma:[tie] to repaire unto y[e] guarde and defence of your Ma:[ts] Tower whensever they should be comaunded.

> Your Ma:[ties] store of muntition &ct: beinge by your Princely providence more royally encreased then ever; The place itself weakned by decaies & defects, do consequently require a stronger guarde then in former tymes. In respect wherof I have in all loyaltie presented unto your Highnes princely consideration theis antient orders, and service-duties before specified. Most humbly beseechinge, that for your better service, your Ma[ty] wilbee pleased to commaunde the recontinuance of theis neglected duties prescribed by former establishements.

Disorders meet to bee reformed

Item it hath byn suffred, y[t] all prisoners havinge the libertie of the Tower might have contynuall accesse of all manner of psons unto them w[th]out nomber, or anie notice taken of their names or occasions of Repaire, A thinge moste dangerous in respect of y[e] smale guarde allowed for y[e] keepinge of a place of suche consequence, and not possible; allowinge soe great a concourse of people to restrayne the trayterous prisoners from intelligence & practice.

It hath alsoe byn pmitted, y[t] all psons Cominge unto a prisoner havinge the libertie of the Tower might contynue w[th] him, in his chamber elswher in meale tymes & in tymes of divine service, the gates of y[e] Tower beinge shoote, and the guarde therof retired, the w[ch] maie give occasion of great inconveniences.

Alsoe prisoners havinge y[e] libertie of y[e] Tower have byn allowed to keepe their wives, & whole famelies ther resident, all w[ch] in meale tymes, & in tymes of divine service have had libertie w[th] in y[e] Tower at their pleasure
The danger wherof is humbly referd unto your Highnes consideration

The warders, minters, & other inhabitants have usually lodged their friends & other strangers, w[th]in the Tower w[th]out anie allowance of the Lieutennt or notice therof given unto him.

There hath also ben suffred a Comon Brewhouse, and Backhouse to bee kept w[th]in y[e] mint, and also a Comon hackney stable to lett horses to heir, whoe have had their contynuall passage, w[th] their Carriages and horses in & out of the great gates, w[ch] beinge very disgracefull and inconvenient I have restrayned.

By means of the newe erected Tenem$^{ts}$ w$^{th}$in the liberties of y$^{e}$ Tower, the inhabitants are so encreased, as ther is not w$^{th}$in the Tower anie place sufficient for their burialls, the w$^{ch}$ tymes of infection wilbe moste dangerous & in other respects very inconvenient.

> It maie therfore stand w$^{th}$ your Ma:$^{ts}$ pleasure, that some place in Eastsmithfield, beinge w$^{th}$ in the liberties of the Tower, maie bee appointed for that purpose.

Decaies necessarie to bee Repaired

Item the Inhabitants upon y$^{e}$ warff, in the Bulwarke and at y$^{e}$ Posterne, have intruded w$^{th}$ their buildings upon the Tower dytche and have bulded noysome houses in the same by means wherof the ditch is muche impayred and the water corrupted
Also yo$^{r}$ Ma$^{ts}$ lodgings and manie other buildings w$^{th}$ in the Tower are in decaye, and maye bee in tyme repayred w$^{th}$ smale chardge, beinge well surveyed and providently bestowed.

The Tower gates & prisoners lodgings are in decaye.
The ancient Sluses & vaults y$^{t}$ weare wont to bee maynteyned to take in water out of the Thames (for strengthninge of the Tower ditche) are nowe utterly decayed.
The Tower ditche beinge the spetiall strength of the Tower, is in great decaye and in manie places landed up to the Tower wall: of the w$^{ch}$ if some repaier be not had, the chardge to your Ma$^{tie}$ will growe excessive.

> It appeareth by your Ma:$^{ts}$ records in the Tower, that the same was repaired by the fines imposed upon the usurers of London, By the w$^{ch}$ recorde the said usurers weare at one tyme fined at 50 markes a peece.

> Some helpe maie also bee added from the inhabitants within the liberties. In respect that the saide ditche is by their default in parte decayed.

The like healpe maie also be added from the Tower Hambletts by waie of men-workes, the whiche I conceave the will willingly performe, if your Highnes pleasure bee to have the restored [*sic*] to their ancient dependancy and priveledges.
And for the remayne which notwithstandinge will amount to a great chardge; your Ma:$^{tie}$ maie be pleased to graunt unto the partie that shall undertake the worke some commission or other sute whiche bee convenient for the performance therof, without anie chardge to bee expended out of your Ma:$^{ties}$ coffers.

> In theis respects most gratious Soveraigne, I haue presumed out of a loyall motive and zeale to yo$^{r}$ service to present unto your Moste excellent Maiestie, this declaration of the state of your Highnes Tower & Castell royall. Moste humbly beseechinge, that out of your princely discerninge Judgement, your Highnes wilbee pleased by waye of Establishment to determine your Royall pleasure touchinge the premisses

> your Ma:$^{ties}$ moste loyall devoted Servant
> S John Peyton

September 1598

[There follow two folios containing Peyton's recommendations for addressing 'Decaies of yo$^{r}$ Ma:$^{ties}$ Mynt & Coynes', which, not referring to the Tower of London in particular, have not been transcribed here.]

# INDEX